NOTES ALONG THE WAY

NOTES ALONG THE WAY

A PILGRIM'S PROGESS

STEPHEN M. BURZI

Red Elixir
Rhinebeck, New York

Notes Along the Way: A Pilgrim's Progress © 2024 by Stephen M. Burzi

All rights reserved. No part of this book may be used or reproduced in any manner without the consent of the publisher except in critical articles or reviews. Contact the publisher for information.

Paperback ISBN 978-1-960090-58-4
eBook ISBN 978-1-960090-59-1

Book design by Colin Rolfe

Red Elixir is an imprint of Monkfish Book Publishing Company

Red Elixir
22 East Market Street, Suite 304
Rhinebeck, NY 12572
(845) 876-4861
monkfishpublishing.com

On the cover: Conscience
"The trunk of this allegorical being represented by a . . . "Bull," means [we] can be regenerated only by [our own] indefatigable efforts . . . That the trunk rests on the legs of a "Lion" means that the said labors should be performed with [a] . . . feeling of courage and faith in one's "might," . . . The wings of the highest soaring of all birds, the Eagle, attached to the Bull trunk, constantly reminds [us] that during said labors . . . it is necessary to meditate continually on questions not related to . . . ordinary being existence. And as regards the strange head of our allegorical being, in the form of the "Breasts of a virgin," this expresses that "Love" should predominate always and in everything . . ."
G I Gurdjieff, *Beelzebub's Tales to His Grandson*, Pg 310
Artist: Alyson Canal-Burzi

CONTENTS

In the Beginning	1
Real Ideas	8
I. Humanity: A Note On Being Human	15
The Left-Hand Path	17
Mankind's Pickle	20
The Duality Of Human Nature	25
Masculine And Feminine Principles	29
The Fruits Of Former Civilizations	32
Hypnotism	36
A History Lesson	39
Black Holes And Bad News	42
Coincidence?	45
A Global Village	48
About Food	51
Genuine Being-Duty	54
Ii. Cosmology: The Study Of The Cosmos	57
In Brief: The Laws Of Seven And Three	59
The Arch-Absurd	62
More About Three Forces	64
That's Preposterous	67
A Relative Understanding Of Time	69

Further Thoughts On Time	71
Scale In The Universe	76
Creating Understanding	78
Pondering On Death	81
Forces In The Universe	84
Changing The Past	88
The Law Of Solioonensius	90
Reflections On Quantum Physics	93

Iii. Common Sense: A Sense Common To All — 97

Consciousness	99
Lying	102
Suggestibility	104
Losing Self-Importance	107
Every Stick Always Has Two Ends	109
Three Injunctions	111
Question Everything	114
Seeing Reality	118
Safeguarding Alarm Clocks	121
The Disease Of Mañana	124
Choosing Your Thoughts	126
Keep Your Brains Clean	129
Requesting Your World	132

Iv. Esoteric Christianity: Esotericism — 135

God's Big Toe (Theory Of Everything)	137
Religion	140
What The Devil?	143
What Do We Owe?	147
Seeking The Kingdom Of Heaven	149
The Holy Family	152

Good, Bad, Sin, Evil	155
Intentional Suffering	157
Christ Died For Our Sins	160
Free Judas Iscariot	162
Successful Prayer	165
Faith And Levels	168
Conscience	170
The Greatest Commandment	171
Beware The Hypocrite	173
Know Thyself	177
Separating Who From What	179
Final Thoughts	181
End Notes	183

IN THE BEGINNING

After some pleasant childhood experiences, my life changed. Long before I ever heard or read the news, I had a sense that something was wrong with the world. Economically, my life was comfortable, though psychologically oppressive and emotionally painful. My mother, God rest her soul, had issues. Yet that was only part of what disturbed me. I felt that there was something wrong with life itself. The premise was off. I didn't have the words in grammar school, but later, I realized everyone was pretending. For instance, my family was in a conspiracy of silence regarding my mother's psychotic behavior. My church and school, which were one and the same back then, were extolling the teachings of Jesus Christ while hypocritically adjusting the rules to suit the occasion—that is, making an exception for that special athlete or long-time parishioner.

The part of the Bronx where I grew up in the early 1950s was drowning in alcohol. Drinking wasn't a rite of passage; it was a way of life. Once in the fifth grade, while I was sitting at my bolted-to-the-floor, cast-iron desk listening to the announcements, one in particular caught my ear. The assistant principal was telling my schoolmates that if they were going to get drunk in the park, they should not wear their school jackets. He didn't say, "don't drink"—though all the children were well underage—he was only concerned with ensuring the school's name wasn't emblazoned across their backs when they did. (Alcohol abuse was so routine in my parish that the high school attached to this grammar school was once thrown out of New York City's St. Patrick's Day parade for excessive drunkenness.)

However, I knew that I was lying too, pretending to like people whom I really didn't like, because I needed something from them—a place to sleep, decent food, a good grade, or a consistent paycheck. I also lied because I wanted people to believe certain things about me—that I was cool, intelligent, funny, handsome, likeable, etc. What I didn't know then was that with extremely few exceptions, everyone was treating me the same way I was treating them.

I didn't like drinking alcohol and instead was drawn to cannabis. Its primary benefit was making my home life bearable. Mom's antics sometimes even seemed funny when I was high. Yet for me, beyond the comic-relief value, smoking marijuana had an entheogenic or spiritual aspect to it, because I glimpsed a place inside of inner peace and harmony. Oddly, I was convinced that this state had to be attainable without drugs.

This idea was confirmed for me the summer before I graduated high school. A girl I was dating handed me a copy of a book she thought I'd enjoy, "Because it's all about drugs." It was Carlos Castaneda's legendary work titled, *The Teachings of Don Juan: A Yaqui Way of Knowledge*, and it wasn't long before I realized that she'd been mistaken. The book wasn't about drugs; it was about the real yet invisible world that gives purpose to life. After that, I knew I had to find someone to teach me how to enter that separate reality that mysteriously exists alongside our own.

At the tender age of fifteen, twin explosions went off in my psychology. That summer, the movie *Easy Rider* debuted across American movie screens followed by the TV series, *Then Came Bronson*. Under these influences, I believed that I could find what I was looking for on a cross-country motorcycle trip. It took a summer of hauling steel rebar at a local precast concrete factory to save up $800, and that fall I started college as the proud owner of a classic 1947 Harley Davidson motorcycle affectionally called a *Knucklehead* by Harley aficionados. This one supposedly had been a show bike—and looked it, painted in eye-catching metal flake colors and all chromed out. I still wasn't old enough to get a learner's permit on my own, so I had to wait.

Though I didn't know anything about motorcycles, I was handy, so I hauled my bike down into a friend's cellar, bought the shop manual and some tools, and began taking it apart, learning as I went. I knew the bike wasn't running because, as I was told, the carburetor was fouled from sitting idle at custom bike shows for long stretches. However, I soon discovered that I'd been cheated. My pride and joy was missing internal engine parts, and some drive-train pieces were worn beyond use. Undaunted, I dissembled the bike, slowly discovering other things wrong or worn out.

I ended up on a five-year plan at college because of a poor choice of majors—I wasn't cut out for Engineering. After two years of intense struggle, I switched to English to get a degree. All throughout school, I was working part time and barely ever had two spare nickels to rub together, so I did all the work on the bike myself, spending my money on parts, tools, and accessories. I finally got the bike running after I switched majors, because I didn't have nearly as much difficult homework to do.

I had it on and off the road a few times, taking short trips to work out issues, then replacing or rebuilding some component that sounded or acted funny, and finally getting it road-worthy—or so I thought. I'd already graduated college, and was working at an upstate-New York residential treatment facility for boys deemed juvenile delinquents, offenders, or PINS (persons in need of supervision) by the courts. I was a prefect—a gentile word for *parole officer*. My role was to provide a stable, safe, and respectful environment to give the boys the best chance of successfully reintegrating into society when their term was up. All I can say about the process is that some you win—some you lose.

While working there I met LL, another prefect. He'd just returned from years journeying throughout Asia. In each place he went, LL exchanged his clothes and goods for local attire so he could blend in and experience that life firsthand. We were each in our own way searching for that invisible world, and when our shifts overlapped, after giving the boys supper, helping with homework, and putting them to bed, we'd get into discussions about the meaning of life that went on late into the night. I was at that job for a little over a year when it finally came time to take my long-awaited cross-country trip.

Originally there were six of us going, but then two dropped out, and eventually, I ended up going alone. Before I left work, LL gave me a copy of G. I. Gurdjieff's book, *Beelzebub's Tales to His Grandson*, as a parting gift, saying simply, "You'll like this." After reading the first three hundred or so pages, two things became apparent: I understood little of what I'd read, yet I was deeply affected by the content. I believed that great truths about the invisible were concealed in the almost unfathomable language; immense concentration was required to even get to the end of some of the almost page-long sentences. Now I knew—I was looking for a school to study this book and learn its secrets.

My motorcycle trip went bust on the first day when my poor packing resulted in a melted taillight that shorted out the electrical system just as the sun was going down. Luckily, I'd installed a magneto ignition system, so I didn't need the power for the engine to run. After a night camping off the side of the road, I limped the eighty miles back to my parents' garage to lick my wounded "builder's" pride.

I became obsessed with restoring my Knucklehead to pristine condition so that it could go a hundred thousand miles without complaint. This led to the discovery of failing bearings in the lower end. I was stuck in New York for the time being, so I got a job with a company in Westchester installing security doors and hardware. It turned out that my motor needed a complete rebuild. For that I had to send it to a shop because refurbishing flywheels and re-sleeving barrels was beyond my capability. As you can well imagine, this was very costly, and my life became a daily grind of a lot of work for little spare money. Almost two years flew by like this, and though my search was still alive in me, externally it was fruitless.

My boss partnered me with a good door mechanic who was also an aspiring musician. He regularly read the *Village Voice*, known as the country's first alternative newspaper, with its finger on the pulse of popular culture. It was also a way for local artists and musicians to meet and find work or *gigs* as he called them. I never looked at the paper—it wasn't my scene, as I had weightier pursuits on my mind.

One day, my partner was out sick, and during lunch—a time usually spent talking and eating—I noticed a copy of the *Voice* was stuffed in a cubby of our service truck. I don't know why, but I felt/hoped/believed that inside I'd find a lead for my search. I carefully went page by page, looking for anything even remotely esoteric. There was nothing. Upon closing the paper in disappointment, I noticed the back page was filled with personal ads. The one in the exact middle read, *Gurdjieff school seeks students, call*... I found out much later that I was the only person who ever responded to that advertisement, which ended its three-week run in that issue.

That was 1979, and at the meeting I'd been invited to I sensed that the two leaders of this Gurdjieff group had knowledge of the invisible world that I'd been searching for. I was assured that they did study *Beelzebub's Tales*, but it was the following exchange that hooked me.

I was asked, "What do you want to do with your life?" I said, "I wish to change the world," full of ideas of how to improve life on the planet. After all, the world needed changing badly. I'd just lived through the assassinations of Medgar Evers, John F. Kennedy, Malcolm X, Robert F. Kennedy, and Dr. Martin Luther King Jr., perpetrated against the backdrop of the war in Vietnam, deadly student demonstrations, brutal nationwide race riots, and the Cuban Missile Crisis.

"What if the world doesn't want to change?"

I was stunned and had no answer. I'd never thought about the world having its own agenda, and that it might be different from mine. The question so intrigued me that I signed up to attend two classes a week for a month, even though they were held all the way down in lower Manhattan, a long way from Westchester. That was the beginning of my formal journey to seek out the invisible world—or inner evolution, spiritual development, bliss, the kingdom of heaven, inner peace... My quest continues today, and these essays are notes that I've taken along the way.

Some essays may seem unfinished, because they're meant to stir the reader's thoughts and feelings, not leave them quietly satisfied with pat answers. Some may sound repetitive—likely, they view an idea through a different lens. Overall, the essays are arranged in four loosely related categories.

If this was a scholarly work, George Gurdjieff's first series of books—collectively called by most readers: *Beelzebub's Tales to His Grandson*—would be my primary source material. Some others include: Carlos Castaneda's first four books of the Don Juan series; the story of Genesis and tales from the New Testament of the King James Bible; Joseph Campbell's collected works, including his radio interviews; the collected works of P.

D. Ouspensky, Dr. Maurice Nicoll, and Rodney Collin; Ancient Greek stories; and some sayings of popular wisdom.

By the way, I took that cross-country motorcycle trip years later for a different purpose, but that tale's for another time.

REAL IDEAS

Our world's troubles are not just what's talked about daily. There're invisible aspects to the present conditions because a number of cosmic cycles are also concurrently ending. People haven't noticed these changes because life is like the story of the scientist's frog.

Long ago, a scientist tried putting a frog into a pot of boiling water to see what'd happen. As can be imagined, the frog fought for its life to get out. Next, he put the frog into a pot full of room temperature water, and the creature sat there contentedly. He put the pot on a burner, and raised the heat in tiny increments over a long period of time. The frog grew accustomed to the slight changes in temperature, and calmly boiled to death. This is our plight today. We're being slowly cooked by a failing ecology; class, race and gender animosity; blind religious beliefs; rabid nationalism; media lies; self-serving political leaders; corporate corruption—the list goes on.

"But what can be done?" is chanted like a mantra, along with its nihilistic version, "What does it matter anyway?" From one point of view, nothing can be done, and we don't matter. The Earth is large, and we are small. Once the planet gets moving in a direction, like a big ocean liner heading for an iceberg, it's almost impossible to stop and reverse course. Yet there's hope. By using an esoteric lens, we see that historically, twenty conscious beings have changed the world before, bringing it back from the brink of complete self-destruction. These twenty are the culmination of the thousands of men and women striving for the same aim.

But how does something like that start? One way to get people going in the same direction is suggestibility. Just about anybody can be talked into doing just about anything if you find the right buttons to push in their psychology. However, that way typically produces unforeseen negative results. You can't fool or coerce someone into achieving self-individuality. One must take the journey because they see the usefulness of it for themselves.

The invisible world is separated from our daily life by our attitudes and habits. These essays can be the starting point for questioning the long-established beliefs firmly holding you down when you were designed to fly. Real ideas show us the invisible world and how it's possible to reach it in this lifetime.

To start, we must take care of our own inner life. If this sounds selfish or antithetical to "higher ideals," know that there's an old saying—to be a good altruist, you must first be a good egoist. This principle is even employed as part of airplane safety procedures. If the oxygen masks drop, you must put yours on first before helping someone else. Real teachers can assist along the way because they can see in a student what they've learned about in themselves and can explain how they overcame or fostered that feature. They can also suggest approaches, though a student is responsible for taking a path or not.

The ancients knew our inner life is our real life. However, our inner life is a cluttered mess. When we meet with an event, we're so busy thinking and feeling about what's going on that we miss much of what's going on. Our thoughts and feelings are more important and more relevant to us than the event we're involved in. As such, we're rarely present to our lives as they pass us by. Experiment with this idea: ask yourself in any given moment it occurs to you, "Am I here now? Am I present?"

If you're rigorously honest, the answer is no. Instead, we're fantasizing about what's happening, has happened, or might happen to us. We're comfortable in our imagination, making small plans about things we'll never do, or being driven to do things that never quite satisfy us, always pushing us on to do the next thing. This lack of presence in our external life is because of an inability to control our inner life—our thoughts and emotions control us.

Sadly, we can't yet stop the audiotapes constantly playing in our heads or the pictures streaming through our hearts about various inner and outer events. This uses up a tremendous amount of our vital energy, which is needed to evolve. Learning to save this energy is the beginning of a lasting positive change of being.

One thing about change—if you want change, you must change. It may sound obvious, but many people say they want to change, all the while secretly wanting to remain themselves and have others change instead. Some wish to change for the better until they get a glimpse of what they must give up to achieve it. Also, there are features in us that are difficult to look at without a strong aim to overcome them. Our inner life is like the infamous painting of Dorian Gray in Oscar Wilde's novel. Yet we must face those disquieting interior truths if we wish to go beyond them. To move up on the scale of consciousness, usefulness, and being, we have to learn where we are on that scale. We cannot start from pretense, lies, and imagination.

There are two paths to inner change: transformation and transcendence. It's of note that transformation, with its ordered advancement through regular steps, is a masculine process, while a feminine process allows for the emotional leaps required for transcendence. This doesn't mean that women can't transform or men transcend—they can. Both paths require real ideas to start.

To transform something in our inner life, it has to be seen in operation, clearly and dispassionately. Then it must be accepted as part of our being without recrimination. Afterward, the feature can be struggled with and made into an ally or left to wither and die. Transcending it requires the same recognition and acceptance, but then, by a mysterious emotional process, one is transported over the struggle to the goal of inner change.

Our planet is in a *Kairos* time—an ancient Greek expression for a time of maximum danger and maximum opportunity. Some of the dangers are obvious; some, not so much, like the one hidden behind the others, affecting them all. Humanity's collective potential is in a state of entropy—meaning the transfer of energy has stopped. Think of a container of hot water next to a container of cold water. By the process called conduction, the hot water heats the cold until both reach the same temperature, and then the transfer of heat (energy) stops—the water has reached a state of entropy.

Entropy is defined as a decline into systemic disorder and randomness (chaos). At this time, it's easy to feel the stifling effect of entropy blanketing our society. Proponents of one side of any issue can no longer hear or relate to those taking an opposing view. Each side is only concerned with propagating their own dogmatic beliefs, thus becoming more insulated and isolated from any other influences. This is the stagnation we feel today, and the reason for our world's current level of chaotic violence.

Oddly, the notion still persists that things will get better in time or with the benefit of some new technology. Sadly, this is not true. A state of entropy cannot be changed without an influx of new energy. But if both sides are unmoving, how is it possible to "heat" things up again?

Real ideas contain phenomenal power. Everything flows from them. For example, the idea of a universe had to exist before the universe could come into being. Real ideas can change perceptions, allowing other possibilities to be seen. The Ancient Greeks called the process *metanoia*—changing one's mind to a broader, higher, finer, and more inclusive perspective.

Real ideas are found in many places, like the adages and aphorisms passed down to us for generations. Sadly, many of them were lost in translation or turned into platitudes and trite sayings. Yet investigating a maxim like *every stick always has two ends* can reveal new depths of meaning that create the needed energy for the journey to enlightenment.

Real ideas do not come from the world of the senses—what we see, hear, touch, taste, and smell—they're from Higher Mind, so their meaning is not easily revealed. As such, there are three conditions for hearing real ideas: a desire to learn, an open mind, and an urge to verify things for oneself. Though some of the words and phrases I use may sound familiar, there are always further depths to be plumbed in a real idea. They are rare and valuable finds and should not be taken for granted, which means, don't allow the wolf to get them. The beast will swallow them whole without tasting the flavors, and excrete them out without digestion. Or as Matthew says in the King James Bible,

> Neither put new wine into old bottles: else the bottles break, and the wine runneth out. (Matt. 9:17, KJV)

Real ideas must be verified in one's life in order to be understood. In other words, they must be experimented with. Otherwise, they'll remain interesting concepts, but nothing more. For instance, the phrase *to pay attention* is an essential idea for inner development. When we pay attention to something we're giving (paying) our vital force to it, feeding the thing—and of course, some things don't deserve to be fed. We have a limited amount of energy at our disposal each day, so we must learn how to shield ourselves from the parts of life that steal it, steering our actions without our knowledge or consent. To say it simply, the less we pay attention, the more susceptible we become to life's draw, which includes advertising, marketing, publicity, gossip, and similar influences.

To take responsibility for our decisions also means not to blame others or circumstances for a poor choice. That's difficult to do in today's society, where finger-pointing is a problem-solving tool, yet we know nothing gets resolved constructively or usefully this way. To take responsibility for one's mistakes (even if only within oneself) and then move on not only relieves stress, it also creates the possibility of working toward a real solution.

Along with this idea is another, "Do your own work." It's interesting to note that most of our prayers ask the Divine to take care of a problem for us. A mysterious proverb from the East tells us to *Pray to Allah, and tie your camel to the post.* Interpreted loosely: God's grace is necessary to accomplish anything, yet we cannot expect the Almighty to do our work for us. We have to do what we can to secure our camel, and pray that the beast doesn't die in the night—something beyond our control.

These essays are meant to evoke in us an intellectual and emotional friction, hopefully eliciting questioning of firmly held beliefs of how the world works and how it might be otherwise. That being said, every philosophy, mythology, and religion has real ideas woven into the fabric of their message. All real truths come from the same High Objective Source, which are then disseminated to different populations, tailored to their times and culture. If we only look on the outside, we only see differences. This is at the root of our misunderstanding of one another and the sense of separation we feel today. To find similarities, we have to see from a higher level. "We're all God's children" is not a catch phrase.

I.
HUMANITY

From the Latin, *humanitas*: human nature, kindness. 1: compassionate, sympathetic, or generous behavior or disposition: the quality or state of being humane
—Merriam-Webster

A NOTE ON BEING HUMAN

It wasn't surprising to discover that part of the definition of *humanity* is kindness—being humane. We possess this trait because of the drop of Divine conscience in each of us.

The highly esteemed American mythologist, Joseph Campbell, (1904–1987), during a New Dimensions Radio interview with Michael Toms called, *The Wisdom of Joseph Campbell,* said to understand that "God is in you . . . is a realization of a spiritual truth through one's life in action." Here lies the rub. Do I truly want to know that God is in me and be responsible for all that entails? Especially if I'll have to abandon some of the cherished habits, piquant tastes, and assorted fetishes accumulated during my time on Earth? In other words, what am I willing to sacrifice to feel Divinity in me?

THE LEFT-HAND PATH

Our educational system is based on memorization: learning by rote facts and notions that panels of experts have determined are necessary for existence. Although they're useful for getting along in the world, they do not represent the limit of knowledge possible for an individual with,

> the boldness to attain the right to be considered by others and to consider [themselves] a conscious thinker.[1]

To think consciously is a journey of discovery, of finding and verifying the truth for oneself. Joseph Campbell touched on this idea when he taught about the two different paths through life. The Right-Hand path is the way of conformity to the rules and norms of society. One is nestled in the comforts of their surroundings, living a successful, dignified, rich, full life—circumstances permitting.

On the other hand, there are those who similarly do their duty to life—earn a living, support others, etc.—yet they have a sense that this is not enough. They feel something is missing in their lives. The ancients called this "Divine discontent," which may take one in search of the Left-Hand path:

> The way of one's own bliss . . . [where] there are no rules, and you will live a life of danger, creativity, and perhaps not a respected life—but certainly an interesting one.[2]

The Left-Hand path is one of self-consciousness, self-direction, and self-fulfillment, where we take responsibility for our decisions and actions. It's the hero's journey. The goal of the Left-Hand path is to bring forth something that hasn't existed before—one's conscious self-individuality.

There is no right and wrong on the Left-Hand path, and there cannot be. Being on the Left-Hand path is a daily test of knowledge and being—a test one faces with eyes and heart open. Like the knights of legend, one lives by a higher code. The striving on the Left-Hand path is to be pure of heart, in service to God first, then neighbor, and then oneself. However, this is not license to do what you wish because, though

> there is no right or wrong on the Left-Hand path,
> there is prudent and imprudent action.[3]

Luckily, regarding imprudent actions, we have a built-in warning system that always gives us a "feeling" about something too good to be true or just not quite right. Then it becomes a matter of our choice. We have to choose our way because the destination is ours alone. We can ask for directions, use signposts, etc.—but ultimately, which way we go and where we end our journey is up to us. There's no one correct way to travel the Left-Hand path, but it's wise to avoid known places in ourselves like swamps of doubt, fear, suspicion, and other quagmires of feeling that drag us down and suck us dry of energy.

Maps can be useful to get a sense of what's ahead and plan a route that possibly avoids these places, but a map is not the terrain. Traveling in our imaginations is easy because we usually underestimate the time and the difficulty of the trip. Once on the road, traveling becomes real as the landscape expands and fills out. The way may be difficult and dangerous, but the views can be spectacular.

MANKIND'S PICKLE

George Ivanovich Gurdjieff (1866?–1949) was a revered spiritual teacher in the first half of the twentieth century. He traveled extensively throughout Asia, Egypt, Tibet, India, and the Far East, studying with various monks, fakirs, and yogis—seeking out the ancient knowledge of humanity's place and purpose in the universe. After many years of immersing himself in this study, he developed a system called the Fourth Way through which one could evolve by their own conscious efforts. The basic tenant of his system is that we do not yet possess individuality or self-mastery, but that it's our birthright to awaken to these higher states of consciousness in us and achieve our full human potential.

Beelzebub, the hero of Gurdjieff's opus, *Beelzebub's Tales to His Grandson*, explains that life began on Earth as the

> result of the erroneous calculations of certain Sacred Individuals concerned with matters of World-creation and World-maintenance.[4]

He says that in the very early stages of our solar system's development, when the Earth was still unsolidified, a comet was making its first full orbit. Due to these "erroneous calculations," the two celestial bodies collided. The impact unbalanced the planet and sheared off a large piece of Earth, which, unable to escape the planet's pull, settled into an orbit and became our moon. (It's noteworthy that modern science now has a similar theory for the moon's genesis.)

Eventually, the planet rebalanced itself on a new center of gravity, and everything seemed to be back in order. Yet there were a number of Sacred Individuals concerned with matters of World-creation and World-maintenance who feared that because the moon was a premature creation, at some later time it could pose a threat to the larger cosmos. They believed the vibrations of smaller organisms would help stabilize the Earth and its new moon's circulation, insuring future cosmic harmony, so they submitted a request to the Lord Creator of All for permission to seed life on the planet. The request was granted, and by fundamental Divine laws, after many millennia of transformations these seeds grew into plants, animals, and us—one-, two-, and three-brained beings.

In essence, life on Earth was initiated to transform cosmic substances into edible vibrations (food) for the Earth and moon to facilitate the flow of energy around them. However, as the three-brained beings continued to develop, these same Sacred Cosmic Individuals grew concerned that mankind's instinctive reasoning was outpacing their understanding. They felt that if mankind prematurely discovered the reason for their existence, they'd perceive it as slavery, which to them would be untenable, and they'd rebel and destroy themselves on principle.

To quiet their apprehension, one Sacred Individual designed and implanted a special organ in our ancestors called *Kundabuffer*. This unique organ had a number of properties, one of which caused humans to see the world topsy-turvy, so they'd never learn their true purpose, thus forestalling any rebellion.

This story is paralleled in an Eastern tale about a magician who had a great many sheep.

> But at the same time this magician was very mean.
> He did not want to hire shepherds, nor did he want

to erect a fence about the pasture where his sheep were grazing. The sheep consequently often wandered into the forest, fell into ravines, and so on, and above all they ran away, for they knew that the magician wanted their flesh and skins and this they did not like.

At last, the magician found a remedy. He hypnotized his sheep and suggested to them first of all that they were immortal and that no harm was being done to them when they were skinned, that, on the contrary, it would be very good for them and even pleasant; secondly he suggested that the magician was a good master who loved his flock so much that he was ready to do anything in the world for them; and in the third place he suggested to them that if anything at all were going to happen to them it was not going to happen just then, at any rate not that day, and therefore they had no need to think about it.

Further the magician suggested to his sheep that they were not sheep at all; to some of them he suggested that they were lions, to others that they were eagles, to others that they were men, and to others that they were magicians. And after this all his cares and worries about the sheep came to an end. They never ran away again but quietly awaited the time when the magician would require their flesh and skins.[5]

The truth behind these tales is buried deep within us, which is why movies like *The Matrix* greatly stir the popular imagination. We sense that we're being kept in an imaginary world, forced to serve a purpose not our own, without our knowledge or consent. It could be said we're victims of that Sacred Individual's miscalculation, but extraordinarily, we are also its beneficiaries. How? That mistake led to our creation, and our possibility of individual evolution through the gifts of free will and choice. We can choose to perform this same assigned work of cosmic balance consciously, gaining enlightenment for the effort.

It's difficult for us to grasp that we're not the center of the universe. It wasn't long ago that an Earth-centered universe was a widely accepted fact. It's still hard to comprehend that we are not alone in the universe. The features of self-importance and false pride are mainly responsible for this feeling: two more of the maleficent consequences of the organ Kundabuffer.

Our lower selves are driven by the needs and desires of life. Our higher selves strive to be intentionally useful to higher levels. Having the choice of which self to follow sets humans apart from other created beings. Angels, those exceedingly high beings, cannot evolve beyond their station. They strive for goodness because they cannot do otherwise. It is said that they worship at the sepulchers of men and women because we've been given the possibility of evolving beyond them.

In opposition is our machine-like lower self, driven by self-love, justification, vanity, judgment, jealousy, imagination, self-pity, false pride, meritoriousness, cowardice, and a host of other traits—more consequences of Kundabuffer. Our essential self is connected to that piece of Divine origin within us, our conscience. That unique seed of individuality can lead to mastery over our lower selves by conscious labor and intentional suffering.

We all think we work hard, yet our inner development requires an extra effort above and beyond what is needed for life. Usually, we must be dragged to a task, be it paperwork, physical work, or psychological work. We believe we've done enough already and these things are cutting into our "me time." Only necessity pushes us to fulfill these tasks, though we often procrastinate to the bitter end, sniffing for our cleanest dirty shirt.

All of our inner complaining to avoid doing something externally or internally uses up energy, leaving us feeling drained and negative. However, going to a task willingly and in good spirits, especially something we'd rather not do (hate doing), actually generates new and finer energies in us as we work.

THE DUALITY OF HUMAN NATURE

What does it mean to have a dual nature? We usually think it refers to there being good and bad in everyone—one whole person with two different sides. Esotericism holds a different perspective. It says that our two natures are actually different beings, and our lower self has our higher self locked away in a prison. This is the idea behind the story of Plato's Cave.

We navigate the world with our lower nature. The wants and desires of everyday life come from there. It has both good and bad characteristics, or more accurately, useful and harmful traits or features. We learn to work, play, raise a family, support our community, and all other life functions from our lower natures. When we wish to know what Divinity wants of us and strive to achieve those aims, that impulse comes from our higher self.

This self supports our wish for inner development while our lower self keeps us distracted by a constant and exhausting tug-of-war for our attention. Our lower nature begins as our guardian, protecting the tender, essential self, but soon it turns into a guard, keeping our higher selves confined in the prison of life while it indulges in its cravings. Yet it'd be a mistake to conclude that our lower self must be defeated and killed. We have to make it our ally, kept under higher supervision.

Since you're reading this book, it can be safely said that you've self-selected to follow a path toward the Good. So, know that our lower nature can help us get there if we learn how to use this part of ourselves correctly. The Jewish mystic and healer, the Baal Shem Tov, regarded as the founder of Hasidic Judaism, taught that we have to lead the devil by the hand back to heaven in order to enter there ourselves.

Individual evolution is the struggle to be consciously useful to the aims of Divinity. For this, a serious effort is required above and beyond what it takes to lead our usual lives. Yet when we make this extra effort to intentionally follow the Good with a touch of delight, it miraculously releases finer energies previously locked up in us—the necessary fuel for a spiritual journey.

Many people don't believe that they asked to be born. They have no idea how they got here, and can't be bothered to find out. If you believe conception is more than simple biology, it begs the questions: From where does a particular spark of life come, and how does it settle in a specific planetary body?

Esotericism teaches that it is a choice, and to some extent, modern science agrees. Of the millions of sperm fighting their way to an egg, yours was the one that beat the overwhelming odds, commencing the phenomenon of birth. Conception is not merely chance but the result of a great effort and choice.

We were given our particular lives because we have something to work out. It can be called an essential flaw, the central issue of our being that we offered to transform once we got to Earth. The problem is that after birth, we're overwhelmed with impressions and forget the starry world we've come from and what we brought with us to refine. This can eventually lead to a sense of something not quite right inside—a vague incompletion or emptiness: a constant reminder we're forgetting something. The question is how to remember what that is?

There is so much commotion inside of us that it's next to impossible to hear our real wishes. One way to hear different things inside us is to practice something not considered useful to our Western minds: sitting quietly and doing nothing.

Strangely, this is quite difficult. We are compelled to do something or we feel that we're wasting time. Children are often in a state of *not doing* until life takes them over, forcing them to "do something useful" with their time.

As an experiment, sit in a comfortable position and do nothing for twenty minutes—don't think, feel, ponder, meditate, pray or anything else—just sit there and be.

Don Juan, Carlos Castaneda's guide to the Toltec's esoteric teaching, explained *Not Doing* as a way of breaking the bonds of our usual worldview, which keeps our higher selves imprisoned. We all have a typical *doing*, the habitual way we feel, think, and act—in other words, our approach to our life. *Not doing* can give a glimpse of other possible ways of thinking, feeling, and doing.

When we believe that we're a particular type of person with certain goals, abilities, and limits—this is our *doing*, which keeps us acting from that usual, habitual self while we pine for a higher and finer life. *Not doing* can help us see that who and what we really are is far beyond the limits of our customary definition and sense of ourselves.

Our higher self is already connected to higher worlds, but we don't know this because our attention is focused on the lower. To make use of this knowledge, we must learn how to persuade the lower self to support that wish. Free will makes this possible. Yet the gift of choice also brought uncertainty, chance, and failure into the world.

Choice means an unknown outcome, which is easily understood if we count the times that we've changed our minds or hearts at the last second. So, choice demands a leap into the unknown, and if we don't make that leap, we remain as we are—static and unfulfilled. However, we don't have to take the plunge alone. Help is always available if we know how to ask. Gurdjieff says:

Any prayer may be heard by the Higher Powers and a corresponding answer obtained only if it is uttered thrice:

Firstly—for the welfare or the peace of the souls of one's parents.
Secondly—for the welfare of one's neighbor.
And only thirdly—for oneself personally.[6]

And it is written that Jesus Christ promised:

Ask, and it shall be given you; seek, and ye shall find; knock, and it shall be opened unto you.[7]

So, our higher, finer life exists now, waiting for us, but we must be persistent in making our request. Individual evolution isn't part-time work. The Lord helps those who help themselves.

MASCULINE AND FEMININE PRINCIPLES

What does the word *mankind* mean? The dictionary defines *mankind* as considering human beings collectively. Yet all human beings are not the same—there are at least two sexes, if not more. The different answers I've heard to this question are mostly variations on the biblical story of Adam and Eve (as related in Genesis 2:21–22, KJV). These weren't satisfying.

At one end of the scale of mankind there is man and at the other end there is woman, and in between are all the shades that make up humanity. The primary physiological difference between the two ends of that spectrum is that women have wombs and men don't. Hence the term *mankind*—different kinds of men, from one end of the spectrum all the way to the womb-men (women) at the other, and all the various sexual identifications in between.

A popular and informative book on relationships between men and women is *Men Are from Mars, Women Are from Venus* by John Gray, a noted relationship counselor. In his book, Dr. Gray explains that when a woman relates a problem to a man, she isn't necessarily asking him to solve it for her. She might simply want to discuss the issue and the surrounding circumstances, or perhaps she's seeking his emotional support or something else. But by a man's innate nature, his first response is to put on a "Mister Fix-it hat" and offer solutions. Most women find this response frustrating. A lack of understanding is at the heart of the misunderstanding.

This miscommunication also happens internally. Though most religious teachings insist that the soul is either masculine or genderless, esotericism teaches that a man's soul is feminine and the soul of a woman is masculine. It's also taught that a man shows a woman where she needs to go, while a woman reminds a man where he comes from. Taken together, this means a man's soul would remind him of where he comes from and what he owes to life, while a woman's soul would show her where she wishes to go and the cost of getting there. A correct attitude toward these reminders can lead us to heaven, while the wrong outlook can make life a living hell.

In Plato's *Symposium*, the playwright Aristophanes (446–386 BCE) explains why people go in search of their soulmates. In primordial times, people had double bodies with their faces and limbs turned away from each other. These original humans were formidable and threatened to overpower the Gods. The supreme God, Zeus, wanted to blast them with thunderbolts, but he didn't want to be deprived of their prayers and offerings, so instead he chose to cripple them. Zeus split these original humans down the middle and separated the two halves far apart. In the millennia since, people have searched for their other half to rejoin their souls together.

The masculine thrusts out, while the feminine takes in. It's the eternal yin-yang, equal and opposite, striving. Yet there is a mysterious third force—the circle that surrounds them, keeping them in relationship. Every couple is a combination of masculine and feminine forces within the unifying force of their relationship. If their connection is mistrust and suspicion, they're held in a dysfunctional partnership. If compassion and trust are the unifying principles, they will share mutual bliss.

As Joseph Campbell said:

> Marriage is not a love affair, which has to do with personal satisfaction. Marriage is an ordeal, and

that's why it's a sacrament.... Each person is giving up their "simplicity" to a relationship in which each person is playing a role. Their relationship then becomes a life-building and enriching experience.[8]

A Note on Human Sexuality—
With the exception of newspaper astrology buffs, most people don't believe that the cosmos influences their lives. Yet our ancestors believed it and understood how our solar system affects both our internal and external actions. One influence they discovered affects the brain controlling our sexual function.

The planet Uranus lies almost perpendicular to Earth, alternately pointing its positive/masculine pole at us, and then its receptive/feminine pole as it orbits around the sun. The planet completes a circuit during an eighty-year human lifespan. Thus, someone born under its masculine influence will be under its feminine influence halfway through their life and die while under the planet's positive/masculine pole once again. Considering this effect over lifetimes—heterosexuality, homosexuality, asexuality, bisexuality, transsexuality, pansexuality, and any other type of sexuality is partly due to this alternating cosmic influence. The same phenomenon can be clearly seen in the related world of fashion, where style continually swings with cyclic regularity from one sexual pole to the other through all the inner changes.

The three primary influences of gender identity are: the cosmic conditions at one's conception and birth, hereditary predispositions, and personal choice. Many indigenous American tribes understood this and treated men and women in nontraditional gender roles honorably, giving them a distinct, alternative gender status.[9]

THE FRUITS OF FORMER CIVILIZATIONS

Ever since their fall, we've heard about the greatness of the Greco-Roman civilization and the benefits we've inherited from them. Much of our philosophy and literature, our system of laws, and even architectural styles like the US Capitol building are all fruits of Greco-Roman civilization. Yet what were the beings of these ancient folk like? When we think of their so-called triumphs, as with all former relationships, we remember the good, while the bad gets swept under the "that's-in-the-past" rug.

For instance, ancient Greece's philosophical Golden Age was the result of one man, Socrates (470–399 BCE). Ironically, later in his life he was tried, convicted, and put to death by his fellow citizens for a charge of impiety: failing to acknowledge the city's Gods and introducing new Deities. It's of note that these are similar charges to those brought against Jesus Christ during his trial. Four of Socrates' well-known sayings are:

- An unexamined life is not worth living.
- Wisdom is knowing you know nothing.
- To find yourself, think for yourself.
- Beware the barrenness of a busy life.

The last one is especially fitting for today's technology-obsessed society, where myriad forms of instant communication fill our lives with busyness. As for the other famous philosophers at that time, as Gurdjieff says, they were, "pouring from the empty into the void."[10] "What! Heresy," you cry. "What about Plato and Aristotle?" Well, Plato is most famous for writing down the words of Socrates, though he didn't heed them. He invented the dialectic method, which is a discussion between two or more people, trying to figure out which one of them is right. This is not putting into practice the idea of knowing you know nothing.

Aristotle was Plato's student, and he followed his teacher's example, drawing on his own knowledge to solve problems. He is called the father of logic, which is the justification of a premise using reason—essentially, thinking you know, and talking until you prove it to yourself and others. To pass any logic course, one must be able to argue both sides of a proposition to a win. In terms of seeking real truth, this epitomizes pouring from the empty into the void. Proof of this can be found in any number of courtrooms where the innocence or guilt of a person is not as important as how well their lawyer presents their case and reasons their position. It's interesting to note that the vainglorious Greek, Alexander, who ravaged Asia, was tutored by Aristotle.

These philosophies have directly or indirectly led to many of our modern "blessings," like the arguments for limitless use of pesticides, plastics, and petroleum products along with those for deploying chemical, biological, and nuclear weapons. Albert Einstein understood the consequences of his theories only after seeing the heartrending devastation nuclear weapons wreaked on the crowded Japanese cities of Hiroshima and Nagasaki. He said, "If I had known, I would have become a watchmaker."

The Roman civilization that we hold so dear was decadent to the core, filled with violence, cruelty, and debauchery. It was built on the backs of slaves, who accounted for as much as 25 percent of Rome's peak population, according to some estimates. The Roman military was especially brutal, having killed by hand with sword and spear an estimated fifteen million people at a time when the world's population averaged two hundred million.[11] That's over 7 percent of everyone living, and that number doesn't include the more than half-million people who met brutal deaths for entertainment in their sports arena, the Coliseum.

Roman debauchery is also legendary. Whole cities, such as Pompeii, were centers for sexual gratification. One of Rome's major deities was Bacchus, god of wine and giver of ecstasy. His feast was celebrated with drunkenness and sexual depravity. Once, the celebrations in his honor grew so out of control that the Roman senate had to step in and tone it down.

We've all heard the names of the Roman elites who made sexual perversion an art form. The most flagrant examples would be the emperors Caligula, Tiberius, Nero, and the empress Valeria Messalina, wife of Claudius. Though these rulers were the most depraved, the idea of living for pleasure seeped into all aspects of Roman life, and their appetites spread throughout the empire and far into the neighboring lands.

The word *pornography* dates back to these times, and this "fruit" of our ancestors is still ripening today. It blares at us from radios and electronic billboards, is splashed across the fronts of newspapers and magazines, and streams across computer, TV, and movie screens. We live in the age of instant gratification, while believing there's nothing more gratifying than sex. This influence continues to flood into our world, drowning human sexuality:

> Forty million Americans regularly visit porn sites, and 35% of all internet downloads are related to pornography.[12]

This is particularly harmful to the young:

> *Among adolescents, pornography hinders the development of healthy sexuality, and among adults, it distorts sexual attitudes and social realities.*[13]

Psychologists [call] addiction to pornography "our most challenging mental health problem."[14]

HYPNOTISM

The dictionary defines *hypnotism* as the induction of an alternate state of consciousness where a person apparently loses the power of voluntary action and becomes highly responsive to suggestion and direction. Its use in mental health therapy is typically to recover suppressed memories or modify behavior.

In *Beelzebub's Tales*, Beelzebub says that humans are the only beings in the universe who can be hypnotized. This is a result of many factors, one of which is the way we're raised. The education given to us by parents, relatives, teachers, friends, TV, radio, the internet, etc., assimilates into our daily consciousness. We never confront this data to verify it, accepting what we've been told because it's been often repeated to us or told to us by someone we trust.

However, according to Gurdjieff's teaching, we also have a subconsciousness, which is an accumulation of what we know through our bloodline—innately passed down to us from previous generations—that has "rubbed up" against our daily life experiences in the school of hard knocks. Our subconscious then is the result of our efforts to turn knowledge into "fire is hot, do not touch" understanding. This consciousness is also said to be the seat of our conscience, our connection to the Divine. Sadly, from our daily consciousness' point of view, the subconscious is only filled with myths, dreams, and nightmares.

The two consciousnesses are disconnected and unaware of each other because if one of them is awake, the other is asleep. One of the results is that if we recognize something "off" in us in our daily life, which is a message from our subconscious, we either quickly forget the perception, or chalk it up to someone else's fault and therefore their problem, or say it's due to circumstances beyond our control. In other words, when we catch a glimpse of something distasteful in our being, we push it out of our minds, or blame someone or something else.

When someone is under hypnosis, they are in fact having their daily consciousness put to sleep as their subconscious is awakened. According to Gurdjieff, this hypnotic state is brought on by a change in the flow of blood, which is not a directional change of the cells' movement, but an activation of the Kesdjan body's blood. (Gurdjieff uses the terms *Kesdjan body* and *Soul* for the two higher-being bodies possible for us to develop. The Christian words *Soul* and *Spirit* are equivalents.)

The aim of inner evolution is to coat the higher Kesdjan body/Soul in us, and then a Soul/Spirit that can become a help to Divinity. We are born with an embryonic soul, which has all the basic functions for life, including a circulatory system. When that blood is stimulated and starts to flow, our subconscious surfaces from its magical enchantment and becomes active.

Our subconscious self is at a young stage of development because we hardly pay attention to it, which may be part of the reason for its openness to suggestion. Hypnosis is proven to effect positive change in some instances, yet because the condition is brought on by someone else, there's often no conscious memory of what took place, so although it may help ease one's life, the experience is not useful for inner development. The soul only grows from our conscious labor and intentional suffering. When the soul's blood is flowing, we're connected to our real life and possibilities.

Hypnosis can help cure addictions to drugs and alcohol that separate people further from themselves, reality, and their conscience, because it makes subconscious suggestions more present (active) in one's daily life.

A HISTORY LESSON

Besides their prolific decadence, greed was another cause of the collapse of the Western Roman Empire. A handful of ruling families had care, control, and custody of the empire, yet their sole concern was to increase their political power and personal wealth. The cost of infighting among Rome's elite was initially borne on the shoulders of foreign slaves and the poor classes of this highly stratified society. Later, the "noble" patricians forced the middle and merchant classes to support their power struggles, which were the political conflicts of the day. After taxes, tolls, and fees drained them financially, the costs fell to the lower ranks of the wealthy, who had to pay their dues to one faction or another to secure their support and/or protection.

The Roman Empire thrived on conquest, draining their enemies' coffers to fill their own. After reaching the limit of their empire's expansion, the government was forced to pay out of their own pockets the expense of outrageous municipal projects, prolific treasury pilfering, and the spiraling costs of the empire's security, maintenance, and repair. All this, plus the upkeep of its expansive military operations, forced Rome to find ways to stretch their dwindling resources. One of the routes they chose was to devalue their currency. Eventually, some coins contained less than 20 percent of the precious metal of their face value. This practice became so widespread that, in parts of the empire, Roman coins were no longer accepted for tax payments.

By the fifth century, the Western emperors were merely

figureheads. The real power was held by the generals of the legions stationed in various parts of the empire, local tribal leaders, and the Catholic Church. By this time, Rome had stopped paying army benefits and often had difficulty paying wages, severely diminishing the status of military service. This lowered their enlistment rates, forcing the government to hire mercenaries. These men were more loyal to their commanders than to Rome, and when problems with their pay arose, some turned against the empire. The last Roman Emperor in the West wasn't ousted from office by foreign powers but by his own hired troops.

The empire's lifeblood was trade, but it soon became less regulated due to widespread unofficially sanctioned corruption. As a result, many foreign diseases rode along with the goods flowing from all over the empire. Thousands died of previously unknown illnesses and plagues, and when essential services to the cities faltered from lack of funds, freshwater and sewer systems broke down, adding thousands more to the death toll.

Rome's fall was a long process that started in the mid-third century. After the empire finally imploded in the late fifth century, a Dark Age descended on Europe that was marked by an intellectual, cultural, and economic collapse that lasted almost a thousand years. During that time, people were worth less than livestock. William Manchester, in his book, *A World Lit Only by Fire*, shows us a medieval world filled with "incessant warfare, corruption, lawlessness, obsession with strange myths, and an almost impenetrable mindlessness."

In light of this, today's headlines show the direction the twenty-first century is headed. Greed and desire for power has caused seventy-nine major wars in the last one hundred years. Up to and including the conflicts in Iraq and Afghanistan, these have claimed over one hundred seventy-five million lives. If we add to this the tally from the ongoing war on nature with its untold deaths by pollution, the deaths from extreme poverty, homelessness, drug addiction, lack of mental health services, poor medical services, etc., we can feel the edges of a similar collapse closing in on us.

Greed is the desire to acquire or possess more than one needs, especially in terms of material wealth. The Catholic saint, Thomas Aquinas, said greed was "a sin against God [because] man condemns things eternal for the sake of temporal things."

> Our culture's emphasis on greed is such that people have become immune to satisfaction. Having acquired one thing, they immediately set their sights on the next thing that suggests itself. Today, the object of desire is no longer satisfaction but desire itself.[15]

This is obvious in the area of technology where the latest device is a must-have, not because it's more reliable and longer lasting, but because it has more bells and whistles—is more attention-grabbing, making more promises for our happiness. If this tendency remains unchecked, we will be unable to be satisfied with anything—ever.

We cannot heed Aquinas' warning by condemning greed in another. Rather, we must strive to overcome our own desires that allow another's to flourish in a conspiracy of silence. This is one of those peeks into ourselves we need to make and ask, "Am I closing my eyes on this feature in others so that they cannot see what *I'm* doing?"

BLACK HOLES AND BAD NEWS

In the early 1970s, an FM station called The Quadfather appeared in the New York City area. It was one of the first stations to broadcast in quadraphonic sound, a cutting-edge technology at the time. Besides being able to listen to Pink Floyd, the iconic British rock band, in what later came to be called *surround sound*, the best thing about the station was that they only reported good news during the hourly segments required by the FCC (Federal Communications Commission).

The station played all the latest and greatest rock and roll and seemed to have sufficient quality advertisers; nonetheless, it suddenly disappeared from the air one night in the middle of their regular broadcasting as if someone had pulled the plug. I couldn't find the reason for the station's demise. Nobody seemed to know anything about it. All things being equal, I posit that their positive-news-only broadcasts were the cause of the Quadfather's passing.

By that time, it had become clear that those in power had a different agenda from that of the average citizen, one that required keeping the rest of the population distracted and living in fear, not unlike the premise of George Orwell's landmark dystopian novel, *1984*. What could be a better distraction than frightening news about terrible coming events? They didn't even have to be true or accurate!

Given the size of the world's population, it's difficult to believe that all the news is bad. There are plenty of distressing things going on in the world and getting worse every day, yet there are also many people striving to help their neighbors, their communities, and the world. Why do we seldom hear their stories and the follow-ups? The "good news" we get is often a soft story, such as an old dog that miraculously survived a seventy-foot fall out of an open window with only a few bruises on its tummy.

Why do we seem to want, and even need, a daily diet of shock jocks, outrageous news stories full of negativity, or vicious biased commentators? Because they're addictive.

> Negative ideas have a very great attractive power.
>
> A negative idea, such as that the Universe is meaningless, can draw millions into its vortex and hold them as in prison. This takes away the chance of individual growth from them and so renders them subjects for mass-suggestion.[16]

A negative idea or action is the psychological equivalent of a black hole—a gravity center that sucks in all the life energy around it. Anyone in contact with a very negative person has experienced this drain. Interestingly, negativity wouldn't have such an attraction if part of our lower nature wasn't seeking it out.

Whether or not we admit it, we're fascinated by and attracted to destruction, corruption, and death. We look for it in our news, podcasts, movies, TV shows, the topics we discuss, and in traffic rubbernecking delays where we slow to a crawl to gape, hoping to see something horrific. We want to view tragedy up close, as long as it's not happening to us or our near and dear. The possibility of a calamity is one of the attractions of professional sports—we're mesmerized by the chance of injury, a fight, an embarrassment or a personal misfortune of their stars.

All types of information outlets exploit this aspect of our

lower nature, and their ability to keep us on the edge of our seats for the unfolding drama of the next catastrophe has made their owners billionaires and us poorer in spirit. Yet *why* do negative emotions attract us? One reason is that people love to complain.

> Many people find it very difficult to refrain from expressing their feelings about bad weather. It is still more difficult for people not to express unpleasant emotions when they feel that something or someone is violating what they may conceive to be order or justice.[17]

This type of negativity has an extremely detrimental effect on our energy and our lives.

> The human organism usually produces in the course of one day all the substances necessary for the following day. Bad moods, worry, the expectation of something unpleasant, doubt, fear, a feeling of injury, irritation... may, in a half an hour, or even half a minute, consume all the substances prepared for the next day; while a flash of anger or some other violent emotion can... leave a man quite empty inwardly for a long time or even forever.[18]

It's work to understand, but when we feel indignant, complacent, self-righteous, self-pitying, meritorious, justified, self-important, and the like—we're being negative. The cure starts with admitting one suffers from the addiction. Struggling to see one's attraction to negativity while not giving in to it can loosen its hold on you.

COINCIDENCE?

Mr. Gurdjieff traveled extensively throughout the East, searching for humanity's place and purpose in the universe, the forces opposing the achievement of that place, and ways of overcoming those forces. He taught a system of inner development, known as the Fourth Way, to thousands of people in Asia, Europe, and America. Later in his life, circumstances forced Gurdjieff to distill his teaching into a total of ten books in three series with the common title of, *All and Everything*. He began writing in the early 1920s and continually rewrote and reworked his first three books of the series *All and Everything, Beelzebub's Tales to His Grandson*, until near the end of his life in 1949. (These books were posthumously published in 1950.)

The premise of *Beelzebub's Tales* is that Beelzebub has been granted a pardon for the sins of his impetuous youth, and he's currently traveling with his grandson to a cosmic conference he's been asked to attend. They're on an interstellar spaceship, and at one point, Beelzebub is explaining to his grandson about the beings living on the different planets of our solar system.

> There is still another planet, quite a small one, bearing the name Moon, in that solar system, my dear boy. Though the beings of this planet have very frail 'planetary bodies,' they have, on the other hand, a very 'strong spirit,' owing to which they possess extraordinary perseverance and capacity for work.
> I happened to notice that during two of our years

> they 'tunneled,' so to say, the whole of their planet
> ... where they are protected from all the vagaries
> of the mad climate inharmoniously changing the
> state of the atmosphere.[19]

Beelzebub's Tales is well known as an allegorical story intended to be the primary study tool for Gurdjieff's teachings. However, undoubtably, there are many levels to his tales and surprising truths about our universe in them. For instance:

> At the close of the Apollo age in 1972, a year before
> the final moonwalk, a NASA researcher argued that
> vast tunnels [must] lie beneath the lunar surface ...
> But the lava [?] tunnels of the moon, like the mythi-
> cal canals of Mars, proved elusive.[20]

Then, in 2009, almost sixty years after the publication of *Beelzebub's Tales*, Japanese scientists, with the assistance of two NASA satellites, discovered "a 50-kilometer long, 100-meter-wide cavern on the moon."[21] To date, over two hundred such tunnels, classified as lava tubes, have been charted, and several groups have proposed exploring them by various means, including using lunar rovers.

Governments with aspirations for lunar colonies are looking at adapting this cavern and other similar tunnels as suitable base stations for human habitation, citing that they would require only minimal additional work to protect people from the dangerous atmospheric conditions on the lunar surface, such as dust storms, hazardous radiations, micro-meteoritic impacts, and the extreme temperature swings on the surface, which vary from 266 °F to −292 °F in its day-night cycle.

Considering the lack of space exploration in Mr. Gurdjieff's time (the first space satellite, *Sputnik*, wasn't launched until

1957 by the Soviets), did he make a lucky guess about the tunnels on the moon or did he find something in the ancient knowledge he studied? We believe that we're more advanced than any previous generation, yet what do we really know of ancient civilizations?

Sadly, we look for answers that keep our self-importance intact, like the belief that alien visitors built the pyramids. But what if we have not progressed since ancient times and instead have fallen from the higher level of being humanity once attained and possibly might attain again under the right conditions?

A GLOBAL VILLAGE

It Takes a Village was published in 1996 by then First Lady, Hillary Rodham Clinton. The title comes from an African proverb that stresses the community's responsibility for child-rearing so that each child has a proper and fitting nature and temperament as an adult. Clinton wrote that children need more than loving families to grow into independent, responsible adults and valuable citizens—they also need safe, respectful, and successful communities.

Today in the United States there are no villages as such. Instead, there are neighborhoods, towns, boroughs, districts, and cities that have become entrenched, belligerent, and intolerant of one another. Everyone is stubbornly sure of the righteousness of their position—often despite their own conscience and best interests. In other words, people's hearts are being hardened to each other. We are like Pharaoh in the following story of Exodus, the first book of the Hebrew Torah, and the second book of the Christian Bible.

The Lord God commanded Moses to go again to Pharaoh, the ruler of Egypt, and urge him to free the "children of Israel" from bondage. Up to this point, God had already sent Egypt eight plagues, including: pestilence, animal attacks, foul water, locusts, deadly hail, and others. After each affliction, Moses had gone to Pharaoh asking him to free the people of Israel. Yet each time, the request was denied because, according to the story, God "hardened Pharaoh's heart." After the ninth plague, the Lord says,

> Yet will I bring one plague more upon Pharaoh, and upon Egypt; afterwards he will let you go hence.[22]

The plague God brings is the killing of every Egyptian's firstborn. And indeed, when Pharaoh loses his son, he frees the Israelites. If we consider this tale psychologically, this hardening of mankind's heart to catastrophe is prevalent today. For instance, almost every month, a violent tragedy happens to our children, sometimes in our own backyard. Sadly, we eventually tune out, saying, "I know it's terrible, but what can I do?" We cannot feel another's suffering unless we struggle to intentionally imagine ourselves in their place, which is a very painful act.

What makes our situation worse is that our plagues are not of Divine origin, but self-inflicted, yet we continue to harden our own hearts to our common global plight. We've given up helping one another, thinking that it's the only way to save ourselves. Humanity cannot blame the Almighty this time for its stiff-neck stubbornness and refusal to change—that's on us.

Mankind stands at a crossroads. Whether or not we can see the bottom of the spiral we've started down, our way of life is in the balance. Ultimately, Mother Nature will recover from the wounds we've inflicted on her because humanity will no longer be a huge factor. Over two-thirds of the population of Western Europe died when the Roman civilization imploded, and they were made of studier stock.

The planet is a living organism, functioning within a larger living organism, which participates in an almost infinite organic body called the *Megalocosmos*—everything that can be seen or sensed in the entire universe. We know leaves can't live separated from trees. Believing that we can live separated from Earth is pure imagination, leading us to a slow, unnecessary death.

If we crack our shells open, and let others in, we'll realize that we're all part of families, which comprise communities that form regions organized into countries in a global population that is dependent on Earth's well-being.

ABOUT FOOD

Typically, we think of food as substances like proteins, fats, carbohydrates, vitamins, minerals, etc.—in various forms that we put in our mouths, chew, and swallow to provide energy to grow, maintain our health, and our life in general. There is a lot of discussion today about the quality of what we eat in light of all the modifications and alterations modern science continues to make to our food. On top of this is the animosity people have developed toward one another over who eats what. Yet there's an esoteric idea that goes above and beyond these debates.

According to Gurdjieff, our human organism takes in three types of food: the ordinary food we eat and drink, the air we breathe, and the impressions taken in through our senses.

> It is not difficult to agree that the air is a kind of food for the organism. But, in what way impressions can be food may appear at first difficult to understand. We must however remember that with every impression whether it takes the form of sound, or vision, or smell, we receive from outside [of us] a certain amount of energy.[23]

The human body can live for days without ordinary food and water, a few minutes without air, but only moments without impressions. This has been proven by the number of "civilized" countries that use various forms of sensory deprivation as torture.

Science knows that our digestive system transforms first food into nutrients the body can assimilate. But there are actually three digestive processes in us to refine the different foods we take in, and this overlap creates various levels of energy. Some go to fuel our physical functions, some to fuel our thoughts and feelings, while some go to feed higher functions that connect us to higher worlds. This is food for our soul and spirit, the finest substances produced in us, resulting from our conscious efforts to intentionally digest the food of impressions.

Our planetary bodies transform the first and second foods mostly without our participation. Breathing and eating maintain life, so the responsibility was taken out of our hands, except for putting food in our mouths. When we breathe, we take in substances that the body needs to sustain life (oxygen, nitrogen, etc.), but also those needed to assist the digestion of the first food, which takes place partly in the liver. There are also particles in the air that go to feed our soul. These particles are also taken in mechanically and only digested part way (if they weren't taken in at all, we'd die). Yet to continue their transformation, or as it's said, to digest them further and refine the energy of evolution out of them, we must be conscious of what we're doing, and doing it intentionally.

This feeling is similar to when we're in a new place for the first time. We have the strange sensation of "I am here, doing this" as we see, hear, feel, touch, and taste new things. This wears off after a while, and we fall back into being in the same old place. The struggle to keep that newborn sense alive, and being grateful for the opportunity while taking in an impression allows them to penetrate more deeply into us to be refined further. This is part of the idea behind saying grace before a meal.

Also, we must use caution when selecting the types of impressions to eat. Taking in coarse impressions like bitterness, anger, doubt, violence, jealousy, suspicion, etc., can poison all three digestive systems. Taking in finer impressions, such as beauty, forgiveness, mercy, sharing, and kindness feeds your soul and helps it to grow.

GENUINE BEING-DUTY

In one of Beelzebub's tales, the captain of their spaceship explains about the marvels of their current mode of transportation and the many beings who worked diligently over long periods of time making great sacrifices to provide what they now benefit from. Hassein, Beelzebub's grandson, is struck by the realization that "everything was not born with [him] like his nose,"[24] and he asks what he owes for these benefits. This is a question few of us ask. Mostly we live our life in the reverse, thinking about how we can get what *we're* owed, or as it's said today, "entitled to." How many of us know that our lives must be paid for?

Although we know that in life something cannot be gotten for nothing, we keep thinking (and hoping) that we will be granted some boon. We say we're "waiting for our ship to come in" or "perhaps we'll win the lottery." We say this even knowing the extremely poor odds of winning. On the other hand, it's an interesting exercise to imagine our lives if we got everything we wanted for nothing.

I remember an episode of *The Twilight Zone*, a science fiction TV show from the early 1960s. A man was a gangster in life, and after he dies, he wakes into his usual surrounding, except now everything is going his way. He has everything he'd always wanted and can't seem to lose at any of his former pastimes—betting on horses, playing cards, and shooting pool. After a few weeks of this he's bored to tears. He complains to his guide, saying that heaven is really great and all, but couldn't he lose once in a while to make it more interesting. His guide asks him, "What makes you think this is heaven?"

When Hassein asks what he owes, Beelzebub says:

> The time of your present age is not given you in which to pay for your existence, but for preparing yourself for the future, for the obligations becoming to a responsible three-brained being.[25]

Hassein, is just starting out on his journey. Regardless of our chronological age, we're in the same relationship to our next step—just starting out. Our time now is best spent learning about the world and ourselves and how they relate and interact. When we see the truth of ourselves and know how we typically react to life, we can make other choices. At the same time, we can grow our connection to conscience, the particle of Divinity in us. If we talk to ourselves, asking the parts of us that habitually lead us away from our aims and wishes to toe the line, it may actually happen.

In another chapter, Beelzebub outlines special efforts that can be made to bring the Divine gift of genuine conscience into our daily consciousness so we can act from it in our lives. They're called Being-Obligolnian-Strivings, consisting of the following five:

> ~ The first striving: to have in [our] ordinary being existence everything satisfying and really necessary for [our] planetary body.
>
> ~ The second striving: to have a constant and unflagging instinctive need for self-perfection in the sense of being.
>
> ~ The third: the conscious striving to know ever

more and more concerning the laws of World-creation and World-maintenance.

~ The fourth: the striving from the beginning of [our] existence to pay for [our] arising and [our] individuality as quickly as possible, in order afterward to be free to lighten as much as possible the Sorrow of our Common Father.

~ And the fifth: the striving always to assist the most rapid perfecting of other beings, both those similar to oneself and those of other forms, up to the degree of the sacred 'Martfotai,' that is, up to the degree of self-individuality.[26]

II.
COSMOLOGY

1a: a branch of metaphysics that deals with the nature of the universe.
1b: a theory or doctrine describing the natural order of the universe.
2: a branch of astronomy that deals with the origin, structure, and space-time relationships of the universe.
—Merriam-Webster

THE STUDY OF THE COSMOS

The dictionary defines psychology as the scientific study of the human mind and its functions, especially those affecting behavior in a given context. Yet we are also affected by cosmic influences that are beyond our control. We seldom see and are generally unaware of these influences and how they affect our behavior.

In the opening chapter of P. D. Ouspensky's book, *The Cosmology of Man's Possible Evolution*, he writes:

> Every system of philosophy and every serious student at a certain stage ... must come to the conclusion that it is impossible to study man without the study of the universe, exactly as it is impossible to

study the universe without the study of man. Man is an image of the world. He was created by the same laws which created the whole world.

IN BRIEF: THE LAWS OF SEVEN AND THREE

In esoteric mathematics, numbers have meaning. Seven plus 3 still equals 10, yet 10 stands for completion or a whole. Thus, we can say that the Megalocosmos is the result of the conjoining of the Law of Seven and the Law of Three.

In the very briefest outline, the Law of Seven is the law of manifestation, or the steps needed for something to be brought into being. This idea is exemplified by a musical octave from low *do* to high *do,* a complete scale where the vibrations have risen continuously until they double. Everything created follows this law, and each note represents a step in the process. There are two places on any octave where the progression of vibrations naturally varies, in between the notes *re* and *fa* and from the note *si* to high *do*. These gaps allow vibrations from other octaves to enter. In other words, these are places where change can occur. For an octave to continue in a straight line from low *do* to high *do*, additional energy must be introduced into these gaps. In terms of an individual's aim, they are the places where an extra effort needs to be made to prevent the aim from deviating.

For instance, when you outline an aim, this is called formulation—low *do*. At the next note, *re*, efforts must be made, and then at the note *mi*, resistance is met. A shock of new energy is necessary for the octave to progress to *fa*, called establishment. At this first gap, the vibrations of our aim naturally slow down. We no longer feel our initial zeal. Here is where most aims deviate, never to finish. If the necessary shock is applied, our aim acquires new energy and for a while seems to be flying along. Then comes the second gap between *si* and high *do*. Here, sacrifice is required—a way of thinking, feeling, believing, or doing has to be given up in order to reach completion. Everything is created according to this law. Learning the nature of each note and how to pass through each is necessary to grow a soul, and requires much study and practice.

The Law of Three is called the Law of Creation, which participates at each note of an octave because three forces are needed to create anything. World creation began with the Divine dividing Itself into active force, passive force, and neutralizing force.

> In the beginning God created the heaven and the earth.[27]

Divinity is active force; that which divides. The Earth passively receives the creative force, and Heaven acts as a neutralizing force mediating between the other two. These three forces combine on every level at every note of every octave, creating everything from galaxies, solar systems, stars, planets, mankind, individual women and men, cells, molecules, atoms, and everything in between.

The three forces are also called masculine, feminine, and a mysterious unifying or neutralizing force. *Family* is defined as a basic unit in society, traditionally consisting of two parents rearing their children. By that definition a "woman" and a "man" are not enough to create a family. The addition of a third force embodied in the "child" is required to complete the triad. This is true regardless of who is playing what particular role.

Likewise, to make bread requires flour, water, and fire; sailing requires a boat, wind, and water; and so on.

Although these laws are inseparable in their operation, they cannot be seen together in their actions. It's like trying to look in the rearview mirror and through the windshield at the same time, yet Gurdjieff teaches that on the path to spiritual awakening, it is essential to understand the Law of Manifestation and the Law of Creation in order to achieve our aims.

One critical characteristic of the Law of Three is that an affirming force always evokes an equal and opposite denying force. Sir Isaac Newton, one of the most influential modern scientists of all time, discovered this part of the Law of Three in the seventeenth century, and called it his third law of motion—for every action, there is an equal and opposite reaction. When I make an aim, life throws up obstacles. If this sounds unfair, consider the opposing force of gravity, without which an aim to walk is impossible. All three forces are necessary, and all three are holy.

THE ARCH-ABSURD

The title of this essay is taken from a short-though-dense chapter in *Beelzebub's Tales*, in which Mr. Gurdjieff delves deeply into the laws of creation and manifestation, forcing the reader to question their usual thinking about how the universe works. He makes the outrageous statement early on in the chapter that our sun neither lights nor heats. He says that in fact:

> Not only does nothing like 'light,' 'darkness,' 'heat,' and so on come to their planet from their sun itself, but their supposed source of heat and light is almost always freezing cold like the 'hairless-dog' of our highly esteemed Mullan Nassr Eddin.[28]

This seemingly absurd statement becomes digestible if we compare the sun's internal and external temperature to our own. The sun's internal temp is estimated to be 27 million °F, while its surface temp is approximately 10,000 °F. Comparing this in a ratio to the human internal temp of 98.6 °F would mean that our skin temp was −460 °F, which is more than a bit chilly.

Science believes the sun feels hotter in the summer because it's 3.28 percent closer to Earth than in winter. How could this slight variation in distance cause differences in temperature from below freezing to above 100 °F on Earth? Not by itself—there are additional forces involved in creating Earth's temperature. This becomes more obvious in these days of global warming as the temp of Earth continues to rise while the sun's energy output and distance have remained more or less constant.

Beelzebub explains that the "heat" we feel does not come to us "d-i-r-e-c-t-l-y" from our sun, but is the result of a process taking place under the actions of the two fundamental laws of the universe, the Law of Seven and the Law of Three. In other words, the heat we feel is a combination of factors, including Earth's position in relation to the sun, the vibrations emanating from the sun and the other planets, the condition of Earth's atmosphere, and which note of which octave the planet is on. This is all more or less grasped by modern science, though not necessarily all together.

Through our conscious efforts and intentional suffering, the universe becomes both more mysterious and more understandable.

MORE ABOUT THREE FORCES

We live in a world of duality: hot and cold, right and wrong, man and woman, yes and no; however, esotericism teaches that three forces are required for anything to be created. The first force is active, the second force is passive or receptive, and the third force mysteriously mitigates the struggle between the other two.

Traditionally, a husband conducts active force—and a wife, receptive force. The child reconciles these two, creating a family. This same principle is true for all families, regardless of who or what assumes a specific role. Sometimes roles are switched, or one person has to play both roles, and sometimes even a pet can be third force, creating a family.

We can see the three forces at work in baking bread, where the flour is passive, being acted on by the water and then unified by the fire. With sailing, the water conducts passive force and resists the boat's movement, or the active wish to sail. The third force of wind is required to mediate the other two forces into a relationship. If there's a good sailor at the helm, they know how to use the wind. But if the captain is incompetent, there's no wind, or the wind sides with the water as in a storm, the wish to sail is in serious jeopardy.

When we delve into the idea of three forces, we find an anomaly. Going for one's aim immediately calls up opposition to it, as if the universe is conspiring against us. But the universe is not out to get us—active force attracts an equal and opposing force because it's needed. We cannot move from where we are without something to move against.

So how can an aim be made in the face of an equal opposition from the universe? The secret is aligning my wish with the third force higher than the opposition of the other two. Throwing my weight to a higher force tips the balance of power because I now have two forces behind my aim. Sailors must acquire knowledge of the wind and the ability to use it properly. If not, third force comes from below, dragging everything down. In other words, when life is third force, it provides every doubt, distraction, and deviation needed for an aim to fail.

And remember, help is always available. If we reach up with outstretched arms to third force, the higher will reach down a long way to meet us. This is how the universe was created—response to request. The biblical story of the Prodigal Son illustrates this idea.

A wealthy merchant's son left his father's home, wasted his inheritance, and ended up starving, eating scraps thrown to the pigs. Finally realizing how far he'd fallen, the son decides to return to his father and repent his sin. He knows he's no longer worthy to be called a son because of his wastefulness, so he decides to ask that he be hired as a servant, for even they fare better than he's doing. He gets up and goes to his father:

> But when he was yet a great way off, his father saw him, and had compassion, and ran, and fell on his neck, and kissed him.[29]

The father ran to meet his child from "a great way off." When any child reaches up to us, it's hard not to reach down and pick them up. And as above, so below—the Father in Heaven will also reach a long way down to help a child who's asking. If our request is sincere in heart and mind, our efforts to reach higher levels are returned a hundredfold by the forces sent down to meet us. This is how the power of life is overcome.

It's a mystery—one must struggle alone on the path to goodness, yet with God, one is never alone. Help is always available, we only need to know how to ask, and then follow the given instructions.

THAT'S PREPOSTEROUS

The dictionary definition of *electricity* is a form of energy resulting from the existence of charged particles such as electrons and protons, which are either held together statically, like in a battery as an accumulation of charge—or dynamically, like current through a live wire. The definition of a *charged particle* is a particle with an electric charge. In other words, science doesn't understand this mysterious power called electricity.

In *Beelzebub's Tales*, we're told that electricity is caused by extracting the positive and negative forces from nature and reblending them without third force. Their resulting unfulfilled struggle creates an electric charge, which we use to power our lights, machines, electronics, and all the other blessings we've created that run on electricity.

The problem is that creating electricity uses up those two forces, and cosmically, they must be in balance in our planet's atmosphere in order for the creative force to properly circulate, and as such provide all the food for the Earth, the moon, and us. The balance of these forces must also be maintained for the coating of higher-being bodies. So, destroying two of these forces by turning them into electricity not only degrades the quality of life on the planet, it inhibits the possibility of our inner evolution.

Although we may not have known of these consequences of overusing electricity, we know that electrical waste accelerates the negative effects of climate change, including higher world temperatures, and the frequency of extreme weather events. Also, the resulting light pollution deprives us of the view of the stars in the night sky, which feeds our wonder about our place in the created universe.

Yet we continue to blithefully extract electricity, feeling like we're doing the right thing. Although it's almost impossible to live without it these days, as anyone who's experienced a blackout can attest to, we must understand the consequences of its criminal waste.

What's preposterous is that the result of overconsumption is all around—and still, we do nothing to rein in these tendencies in us. A simple way to curtail this misuse is one your parents probably often said—turn the lights off when you leave a room. Also, when in the room, ask yourself if there's enough light with the sun in the windows or must I turn on an electric light to see what I'm doing? They're not big efforts, but they'll lead to an increase of consciousness.

Not long ago, and for many millennia before, the world was lit only by fire. Why is anything more than emergency lights necessary for our empty buildings? Why do we need to see them lit up all through the night? Why can't streetlamps and highway lights be designed to serve their purpose without having to illuminate everything for hundreds of yards around? At night from space, our planet is lit up like a gaudy lighting-shop display window. Are all those lights useful and necessary?

Even now, we're creating even brighter lights, which will probably blot out the few stars still visible in the sky. Generations are growing up without the beauty of the Milky Way and the wonder of the constellations in their lives. Is this a price worth paying to see flashing electronic billboards 24/7?

A RELATIVE UNDERSTANDING OF TIME

Simply put, time is relative. Gurdjieff tells us that objectively time does not exist, it's a uniquely subjective experience. The measurement of passing time is always some fraction of a higher cosmos' time. In other words, time is measured by cosmic events surrounding a particular being. For instance, we call one year the time it takes the Earth to make one full rotation around the sun—approximately 365 days. If we lived on Mercury, a year would be only 88 days long, on Mars, it would be 687 days long, and so on. Objective science marks standard time measured against the duration of a particular Divine event on the Most Holy Sun Absolute. Yet that is still subjective for the beings there.

The time we're most concerned with is the time of our lives, yet according to Gurdjieff, that time had to be altered by Nature because of the poor quality of our vibrations. In ancient times, when people lived more in accordance with the principle of Reciprocal Feeding, they lived long enough to grow a soul. However, humanity's vibrations had so degraded that they only became useful to the local system. In other words, mankind didn't vibrate at a fine enough level to feed higher worlds. Instead, they were on par with one- and two-brained beings, and their lifespans were set accordingly.

This trend has continued up to the present. Although it's not necessarily proof of this idea, there's an interesting correlation to the book of Genesis in both the Christian and Hebrew bibles. Before the flood, some men reportedly lived up to nine hundred years. Afterward, the longest lifespans were only one-hundred-and-some years. As we strive to evolve, the fineness of our vibrations increases, and we become more useful to creation, so our allotted time to evolve lengthens, measured in work done.

FURTHER THOUGHTS ON TIME

Gurdjieff called time the "Unique Subjective."[30] This is not different people feeling time passing either more slowly or quickly. This idea refers to the different scales of time on different levels of the Megalocosmos. Mr. Gurdjieff also said that time is breath—as a way of measuring and comparing these levels.

P. D. Ouspensky (1878–1947), a Russian philosopher and close student of Gurdjieff, recorded and expanded these ideas in his book, *In Search of the Miraculous*. He created a table that relates levels of the Megalocosmos to each other by their times. For example, close to one end of the scale, we note that a mayfly is born, matures, mates, grows old, and dies in about a day—living the equivalent of our eighty-year life in twenty-four hours. Closer to the other end of the table, if we take all of nature together, her trees and foliage can be said to exhale oxygen during the day and inhale it at night. Designating this as one full breath in twenty-four hours and calculating an average of 23,040 breaths a day for man, Nature's day is approximately 63.12 of our years long.[31]

From this, we can better see our relationship to Earth. We are like specks on a spot on the planet. Still, since the Industrial Revolution of the 1850s, we've done a lot of damage to Nature. Taking scale into account, what we've done in the past century-and-a-half is a few days for Nature. In that time, we've gotten her sick, and the questions we need to answer are how bad will the illness be, and how long will it last? It may take generations of our time for Nature to heal, yet we continue to abuse our hostess.

* * *

A being's time can be calculated by the events in their life. In other words, our lives can be measured in work done as opposed to duration. If we compare life to a spinning top, we see that in early childhood, many revolutions are completed in one measure of time. This is why we marvel at the energy children have. During the course of living, the number of revolutions or the amount of work done begins to slow until the top stops spinning and falls over in death.

If we want to live a full, thrilling, and sometimes possibly dangerous life, we have to spin faster. Someone like Leonardo da Vinci lived hundreds of years as measured in accomplishments. When we're living in a higher, finer place in ourselves, we're also in a higher, finer time (spinning faster).

This was an important question for me when I began to study formally for a period of time. I had to ask, "Is there time for me to do what's necessary?" After all, I didn't want to start and then die before finishing. I was told that if I learned to use all my brains when I had real work to do and remembered that the needs of life only required a pinky's worth of effort, then there would be time enough.

* * *

Ouspensky posited three dimensions each of time and space, making six dimensions of reality.[32] He called the first dimension of time "passing time"—the line of our life from conception to death. The second dimension is eternal repetition, or Eternity, which extends perpendicularly out from the line of our life, creating a two-dimensional plane.

This is the plane of our existence, which can also be viewed like many power lines, strung one above the other on poles along the roadside. The wires close to the ground carry the least voltage. The lines carrying higher voltages are higher up. This means that if we wish for a livelier life, we need to leap up to the next wire.

To make that leap, you must know where you are. If you leap in imagination, you'll land there. The difficulty is that we're only dimly aware of the present moment unless someone draws our attention to it. In our typical state, we "sort of" know we're here now, "sort of" remember a moment ago, and "sort of" feel the next moment coming, but it's all "sort of" vague. The ancients taught that our birthright is to know the time of our lives—past, present, and future—and know we can make changes in all three.

This is possible by making conscious efforts toward an aim and suffering intentionally to see them through. This means going beyond oneself to step up into the life waiting just above us. This idea is connected to real faith.

* * *

Eternity is typically thought of as an unending line of time. Yet there are no straight lines (octaves) in the universe without additional energy input. Left on their own, all lines eventually become circles. This is also true for the line of our lives, our first dimension of time. The second dimension turns that circle into the disc of our eternity. In Ouspensky's third dimension of time, the disc is spun on its axis, becoming a sphere or a three-dimensional solid. Not a solid as in unmoving and fixed but in that all its points are connected, making a unified whole.

In other words, in this dimension we have access to our entire life—past, present, and future—simultaneously. Ouspensky calls this "the world of all possibilities."

This philosophical idea parallels the scientific discovery in the field of quantum physics called Superposition. The scientists found that as they observed a tiny piece of matter moving at breakneck speed, it acted as expected, like a particle. However, when they weren't watching, the matter exhibited properties of a wave, meaning it wasn't in any particular place but in a wave of potential positions. One meaning of this is that by consciously participating in our lives, we can choose the one we wish to live.

* * *

We've all had glimpses into higher times, be it déjà vu or a premonition. This is a brief moment when we experience a slice of eternity—past or future instances of the moment of time we're in. Deep in our gut, we know that these rare experiences are real, and are proof of other lives. Yet in the day-to-day, we still believe the future hasn't happened and the past is gone. However, this idea of a third, solid dimension of time means that all our past is open to examination and change, and our future awaits present choices.

* * *

Don Juan was a Yaqui Indian Medicine man who showed Carlos Castaneda the esoteric teachings of the Toltecs. There was one lesson he called the "cubic centimeter of chance." Don Juan said that to grasp our fleeting chance before it passes, we must be aware... alert, [and] deliberately waiting, [in order to have] the necessary speed, [and] the prowess to pick it up.[33]

We make jokes about opportunity knocking, but we have to be ready to answer the door. Kairos time, or "God's time," is not measured in hours and minutes but by its value and quality. It's the perfect moment to act, when change is possible.

SCALE IN THE UNIVERSE

We're all familiar with the sometimes friendly, but more often hateful, object on the bathroom floor. This is one kind of scale. Another type measures relative vertical relationships, like comparing the DNA of vegetables, animals, and humans. We supposedly share on average 50 percent of our DNA with plants, even more with the animal kingdom, and in the ninety-percentile range with apes. In the same way the Cosmic Scale is a ladder through the Megalocosmos, relating worlds to one another. It also shows where a single individual and humanity in general fit into the scheme of things.

There are different measurements to locate position on this vertical scale. One of these is usefulness. A case can be made for the sun being more useful than the moon. The sun supports the entire solar system, including the moon. But as far as life on Earth goes, it could not exist without both of them.

Trees refresh the air, producing much of the oxygen we breathe. They provide food and shelter for birds, animals, insects, and building materials for mankind. As firewood, they keep us safe, warm us, and cook our food, improving our quality of life. Rocks are strong, stable, and durable, and we also build with them, but they're harder to use, and their uses are more limited. So, on this scale of usefulness, trees can be said to be higher than rocks. There is no judgment here; both are needed to complete life on Earth.

Humans have a place on this scale both as a species and as individuals. However, an individual human's place is not like other beings. Trees are always trees, and rocks are always rocks. Thanks to our dual natures, men and women are born with the possibility of evolving to higher levels of usefulness in the Megalocosmos. Although, depending on where we throw our weight, we can also devolve until finally, like the character in Ibsen's play *Peer Gynt*, we're taken to the button-molder and melted down to be recast.

We're all aware of different levels within ourselves. It's in the common saying, "Come up in yourself." When in a holy place or a place of singular beauty, the higher in ourselves we are, the more deeply we can take in the fine impressions around us. When we're negative—in a place of annoyance, sentimentality, complaint, and so on—we see only the refuse spilled on the ground around an overfull litter basket at the entrance to the Acropolis. We complain bitterly about "those pigs" (which is true—litterbugs are slobs), but it blinds us to the beauty all around, and we miss the higher for the lower. When we can see both, we can choose to put our energy into the finer aspects of our life, feeding our higher selves.

Although scientists proved centuries ago that the world is round, the idea that it's flat is making a comeback in some circles. This erroneous notion stems from an inability to see levels, a type of blindness that makes one believe everything that *looks* similar *is* similar. Yet the old saying, "Don't judge a book by its cover," was true before the invention of books. To see another requires looking from a higher place in yourself.

The higher up in yourself you are, the more you can see around you, and the more inclusive your view. Divinity sees from on top, looking down on and embracing all of Creation. Inner evolution is rising up this scale in emulation of the Divine. Only by raising our perspective and broadening our worldview can we take in more of the beauty around us, which, when properly digested, releases the energy necessary for spiritual development.

CREATING UNDERSTANDING

> Man has in general two kinds of mentation: one kind, mentation by thought, in which words, always possessing a relative sense, are employed; and the other kind, which is proper to all animals as well as to man, which I would call 'mentation by form.'[34]

The difference between these two types of mental processing, loosely translated as thinking/perceiving, is illustrated in a story from *Beelzebub's Tales* about a young Transcaucasian Kurd. This traveler sees some beautiful fruit in a fruiter's shop, and finding the price "not at all high," buys a whole pound with his last few cents. He eats them for lunch, and after almost bursting into flames, we discover that the fruit "fancied for their appearance alone" was the "not to be joked with noble red pepper."[35]

The man assumed the "fruit," like others he'd eaten, would be sweet and juicy—mentation by form. But according to mentation by thought, we know that fruit is the part of the plant that develops from a flower and contains its seeds. Some examples are tomatoes, pumpkins, cucumbers, olives, pea pods, beans, nuts, corn kernels, and peppers. Most of these have a sweetness to them, but not like nectarines, plums, and pears, which are sweet by their definition. (Note: Vegetables are the other parts of certain plants—leaves of cabbage and lettuce, stems of celery, buds of cauliflower, and roots of potatoes, onions, and carrots.)[36]

Joining mentation by thought to mentation by form creates understanding. Anyone who's ever eaten a hot red pepper, like it or not, will never forget the experience, but they won't understand why the "fruit" tastes that way until they know the definition. Then the next time they look for fruit, they will not buy on looks alone. Understanding is in one's being forever.

Ask ten people to define a man, and you'll get ten different answers. From the viewpoint of a religious person, it's about being a saint or a sinner. Business people think of financial possibilities. Military people see in terms of having served. Astrologers see in terms of zodiacal signs. Politicians see in terms of voters or donors, and appear to their constituents as taking their community to higher standards or as scoundrels, misusing their power and position for their own advantage and privilege.

All these definitions are about outward behavior. At the present time, we're unable to see inside an individual's mind and heart to know their struggles and wishes, so we define them by what we can see. Yet in a Kairos time like ours, zealots can become saints, as on the mount of Golgotha where Jesus Christ was crucified.

Being absolutely sure that things are exactly the way we see them underlies all miscommunication and misunderstanding. Our worldview is so deeply ingrained that we assume others see the world as we do—and insist they must if they don't. The first step to understanding another is to hear what they're actually saying. The difficulty we encounter here is that,

> We listen to our own thoughts when learning, therefore we cannot hear new thoughts...[37]

Here's an experiment: while listening to someone speak, ask yourself, "Am I hearing what this person is saying, or what

I think they're saying? Am I hearing their thoughts, or assembling my own and waiting to voice my opinion on the subject?" Usually, we're so involved in what we want to say and how we want to say it, that we're deaf to what the other is saying.

Another feature of our lower nature that makes it difficult to hear is our need to always be right. We see this feature at work especially in child-rearing. Parents always think that they're supposed to know all the answers to their child's questions, even when they're not familiar with the subject. It's bred into us. I've caught myself doing it.

It's quite painful to admit, "I don't know," especially to your child. It somehow makes us feel less competent as parents. Strangely, it's even harder to follow up with "Let me find out," and then doing the research. However, this way, you teach your child how to question and search for answers as you discover something new about the world and yourself.

Understanding requires an effort to go beyond what we've been told or been educated to think. It requires time to investigate a subject and then apply the knowledge in one's life. This "trying on for size" joins one's knowledge to one's being, which creates understanding. This is necessary if we wish to evolve into what we were created to be—helpmates for the Divine.

PONDERING ON DEATH

In the *Mahabharata*, the esoteric Indian saga of war and destiny, there is the story of five brothers who are all married to the same woman. They are tricked by their cousins into wagering her, and they lose. For the sake of love and honor, they must now rescue her from them. Along the way, their character, resolve, intelligence, and fortitude are sorely tested.

During one such trial, each of the brothers is near death from thirst when one by one, they come upon a lake. Before being allowed to drink, they have to answer a riddle. When the last brother arrives, his four siblings are already dead. He's told of the conditions for drinking and then asked, "What is the greatest marvel?" The eldest and wisest brother replies, "Each day, death strikes [yet] we live as though we were immortal. This is the greatest marvel."[38]

His correct answer allows him to drink and also restores his brothers to life. It's difficult to entertain thoughts of one's death. "How morbid," we say, or "There's time enough for that," we think, because something refuses to consider the possibility of us dying—a great marvel indeed!

* * *

Don Juan speaks of using Death as an advisor:

> Ask Death's advice [about everything] and drop the cursed pettiness that belongs to men that live their lives as if Death will never tap them.[39]

Don Juan is telling us to consider our death as we perform our acts on Earth. Think about it—if this is the last time you are ever going to do something, how do you intend to do it? Will you make it the finest it can be? This is a possibility if we take don Juan's instructions, living each moment as if it was our last chance to do a piece of work—externally or internally.

We don't live our lives this way, and we marvel at all those prolific people like Mozart, Shakespeare, da Vinci, and others who must never have slept. Conversely, we believe we have all the time in the world to change, and of course we will do much more and better-quality work—tomorrow.

* * *

One of Beelzebub's tales is about humanity's history of war, crime, and unnecessary suffering. His grandson asks what those beings can do to correct these unbecoming conditions on Earth. Beelzebub replies that the only solution is that:

> every one of these unfortunates during the process of existence should constantly sense and be cognizant of the inevitability of his death as well as of the death of everyone upon whom his eyes or attention rests.[40]

Knowledge of our death is the stroke that makes our life real. What more can we do to live each moment to the fullest and make our lives more cosmically important, except to realize that our time for doing this work will end?

* * *

Death is life's ultimate truth. It's terrifying because of our fear of the unknown, and also because when we're dead, we'll be missing life. And we're very attached to the perceptions of our five senses. Yet this assumes that death is a cessation of living. Those looking forward to a long nap may be disappointed.

Rodney Collin (1909–1956), a student of Gurdjieff and Ouspensky, wrote *Theory of Eternal Life*, expanding on the idea of three dimensions of time. In the chapter, "Lives Between Death and Birth," he says:

> It is possible to [conclude], as we have done that the moment of death and the moment of conception are one.... This occurs because the energy of death and the energy of conception are of the same intensity and subtleness.[41]

Our real lives have the possibility of extending far beyond the time spent physically on this planet because of the chance to coat higher celestial bodies inside this planetary shell. Yet oddly, if we think of our souls at all, we think of them as already complete inside us but separate from our daily life. We typically only take our soul out to clean and polish once a week to be ready for the next week.

Our soul, no matter at what stage of development, plays no part in our daily life because it's not in our daily thoughts. This causes us to wonder what the soul is and where it flies off to when we die, always hoping for some heaven or fearing an equally mysterious hell—but we don't know.

We must consider the inevitability of our death in order to begin to understand the meaning of our life.

FORCES IN THE UNIVERSE

> Everything existing in the world falls to the bottom. And the bottom for any part of the Universe is its nearest 'stability,' and this said 'stability' is the place or the point upon which all the lines of force, arriving from all directions converge. The centers of all the suns and of all the planets of our Universe are just such points of 'stability.' They are the lowest points of those regions of space upon which forces from all directions of the given part of the Universe definitely tend and where they are concentrated. In these points, there is also concentrated the equilibrium which enables suns and planets to maintain their position.[42]

In the above passage, Beelzebub is explaining the Law of Falling to his grandson, who has asked how their ship can cross the vast intergalactic spaces through which they're traveling. The Law of Falling is not the law of gravity, which is only one of the forces he mentions. Gravity is a weak force in the universe, as its effects lessen with distance, an idea we grasp as weightlessness in space.

These "lowest points" attract all of the lines of force, including electrical, magnetic, gravitational, and nuclear forces, as well as various cosmic and psychic emanations and radiations, including the actions of the laws of Three and Seven. According to Beelzebub, where all these forces meet is where they concentrate into the point that maintains a celestial body's orbit.

Einstein's attempt to describe all these forces as "gravity in space" also falls short of the Law of Falling. He wrote:

> Consider if the 3-D universe was a flat, 2-D sheet. Each object in space acts like a ball that weighs down on the "space-time" fabric and creates a bulging pocket similar to a shallow depression in the ground. That curvature of space-time has an inward falling effect on the paths of other objects.[43]

However, when we add in the movement of the bodies in three-dimensional space, the model doesn't hold up because the sheet becomes a solid. So instead, we can imagine a huge see-through box with a miniature universe suspended inside. Now consider the spiraling movements of all the celestial bodies within as they circle larger bodies, which in their turn are traveling through space circling around even larger cosmic bodies. What is causing all that motion?

Even assuming that somehow gravity is holding things in relation to one another, how and why are all the celestial bodies moving in the first place? According to modern science, a big bang set everything in motion, and as for keeping things together, they tell us that only two forces are needed to keep one body in orbit around another. The first force they say is of course gravity, the attractive force between bodies. A second (mysterious) force propels the lesser body tangentially away from the larger one.

> A spacecraft counters Earth's downward pull by creating enough horizontal speed so that it continually slides sideways as it simultaneously falls toward the

planet, creating an orbit. For instance, the space shuttle typically travels at a blistering 17,000 to 18,000 mph around the Earth to stay aloft.[44]

Our solar system is traveling through space at 12 miles per second (over 43,000 mph) with all the planets and their moons simultaneously circling the sun on its journey. One can imagine a solar system leaving long, gracefully spiraling trails as it journeys through the cosmos. That can't just be various rocks and balls of gas haphazardly moving through space. So, how does the moon or Earth or our solar system, for that matter, generate the necessary speed to stay in an orbit, keeping precise positions?

Celestial bodies appear to be in a delicate dance, negating the possibility that the cosmos is an unconscious mechanism. However, if everything *is* just a part of an immense clockwork of unknown origin, built for an unknown purpose, we must admit that the Designer worked at a level of intelligence far above any possessed by those of us trying to figure it out.

So, what forces keep the cosmos going? To answer this, we have to think differently about cosmoses. A cosmos is defined as a living organism that requires food, air, and impressions. Each cosmos is living within a higher cosmos, and each is born and will die in its time. According to Gurdjieff, the highest manifested cosmos is called the Megalocosmos, which is the body or the dwelling place of the Unmanifest Creator. This is the same for us, an unmanifest force animating our physical body until it leaves us at death.

Quantum physicists have discovered part of the truth that the universe is alive and interconnected. If you stretch your mind further, you might imagine all the suns as part of the solar plexus of the Megalocosmos. Classes of galaxies could be parts of its vital organs, and the circulation of energies around the universe equal to our circulatory, lymphatic, and nervous systems sending messages throughout the body. It's not such a great leap when we account for scale. Celestial bodies are pulsing with life in varying degrees and communicating with one another as the parts of our bodies do. These are the sounds of the universe that modern scientists can now hear. "As above, so below" is an ancient esoteric saying. An interpretation of this idea is that the only pattern Divinity had for creation was Itself, so all creations are based on this Divine design. This is one meaning behind the saying: "God created man in his own image" (Gen. 1:27, KJV).

CHANGING THE PAST

Thinking of time as a straight line leaves us looking ahead, hoping for or fearing what is to come—or looking back, lamenting or glorifying what has passed. We accept that our actions in the present affect our future, yet we believe our past no longer exists—both our good moments and regrets are already set in stone. But Esotericism and quantum physics agree: human beings can affect their present, future, and past.

Quantum physicists have experimentally proven that time flows forward, *and* in reverse—called *time-reversal symmetry*. Monitoring a patient's brain functions as they underwent surgery, the attending physicians and specialists noticed that when the patient's toe was stimulated, the signal appeared first in the brain, then was sent to the toe in reverse time, so for the patient, the toe felt the pinprick first. Though infinitesimally small units of time were being measured, the findings were conclusive.

The ancients taught that the nature of time is cyclic. Some of you might be familiar with one reference to this. In 1965, an American rock and roll band called The Byrds set the biblical Book of Ecclesiastes to music in their hit song, "Turn! Turn! Turn!":

> To everything, there is a season, and a time to every purpose under the heaven:[45]

The Buddhist idea of the Wheel of Time represents life's eternal repetition. Another is the ancient Egyptian symbol of the Ouroboros, the snake or dragon devouring its own tail, which the Alchemists in the Middle Ages adopted for their representation of eternity. We're also reminded of eternal repetition in the hours, days, weeks, months, and years of our lives—filled with all the dramas, tragedies, and comedies that we repeatedly experience.

This circular nature of time allows us to see what's gone before, since it's not lost behind us but tangential to us and also ahead of us. This makes our past both accessible and alterable, meaning that we can go to a specific time and place in our life and transform or transcend a particular moment.

The first step is accepting the truth of that moment. This allows us to choose a different response and imprint that on our past, making a change in our present and future time. It takes a deliberate emotional effort to see the truth of oneself without justifying or judging—yet imagine living the life you wish for.

THE LAW OF SOLIOONENSIUS

We're always sending and receiving vibrations to and from people and things around us. Interestingly, we only notice this phenomenon when it evokes an obvious response like when we're thinking of someone and they suddenly contact us "out of the blue." Scientists studying the invisible connections between people have verified that communicating thoughts and ideas by a means other than the known senses is possible because, by design, we're vibrationally connected.

We have cosmic receptors as well. Some influences come to us as laws—like gravity, breathing, eating, sleeping, and many others of which we are unaware. If we can see the number of influences we're under, we have a chance to free ourselves from some of them. One of these influences Gurdjieff called the Law of Solioonensius, which he discovered in a unique way.

> Of the name alone of such a law, I happened to learn for the first time, when still very young, from a certain very ancient Armenian papyrus, and the details of this law I accidentally cleared up many years later, during my study of the so-called 'map of pre-sand Egypt' which had come, also altogether accidentally, into my possession.[46]

Solioonensius is the name of a cyclical cosmic event where two celestial bodies come close enough to one another so that their forces begin to affect each other, making them strain to stay in their orbits. Many of us are familiar with this sensation, which is similar to a stranger approaching us too closely on the street. We feel agitated because, as commonly said, we feel they're invading our personal space. We tense up with our nerves on edge. Will they bother us? Cause us harm?

Celestial bodies feel that same tension. However, because of the difference in scale, what they feel as a passing moment, we may feel for months or even years on Earth. We sense this planetary tension as nervous energy, which has two effects on us. In the lower nature, it feeds anger, violence, crime, civil unrest, and war. For a man or a woman striving to raise their level of being, that tension can energize one's aim because it also evokes,

> the feeling of religiousness, namely that 'being-feeling' which at times appears in the desire and striving for . . . speedier self-perfecting in the sense of Objective reason.[47]

If we pay attention, we can sense that the world's present state of agitation has a cosmic aspect. Some effects Solioonensius has on our planet are virulent patriotism verging on fanaticism, religious zealotry, self-righteous extremism, widespread bigotry, and systemic persecution of segments of the population that result in explosive outbursts of violent revolution.

There was a time not long ago when people spoke about expanding their consciousness, and peace and love occupied a psychological space in the public's mind. Now, not so much. We have shrunk to living in isolated, insular groups, believing our propaganda while being suspicious of everyone else.

So how is knowing the effects of this law helpful? First, verify the idea for yourself. Do you find yourself more agitated all the time these days? Are you getting mad at the smallest things and feeling generally pissed off? Are you quicker to argue, and do you fight more often? Now look at the world—do the same feelings seem to be coming from practically everyone? That's a sign of a cosmic influence, making it less personal, loosening its grip on you. This means that when you experience the effects, you can choose not to go with them. Of course, this takes practice.

REFLECTIONS ON QUANTUM PHYSICS

Note: many of the connections in this essay sprang from watching the 2004 film *What the Bleep Do We Know!?*, which posits a definite spiritual connection between quantum physics and consciousness.

Quantum physics is breaching boundaries between science, religion, and philosophy. It's been "discovered" that on the level of the tiniest particles of matter making up the known universe, everything is entangled. Matter in one place in the universe has an effect on matter in another, depending on certain factors like focus, intention, and intensity. It's not a spiritual euphemism, but a scientifically repeatable fact that telepathic messages can be received by the intended person. They've also shown them to be able to change prerecorded tapes, raise the quality of water, change its pH level, and other amazing things.

We affect the universe around us and can alter our life by altering how we respond to life. We either put out positively or negatively charged vibrations. It's a struggle to put a positive vibe into the world, but not making the effort increases our world's already overburdened negativity. We can choose to increase the chaos or struggle against it. The middle ground doesn't last long.

* * *

Quantum physicists have "discovered" that the universe is an organism, extending infinitely in time and space, like a giant *Cosmic Being*. It's animated by an unmanifested force the way our planetary body is animated by an equally mysterious spiritual entity. Like every other type of being, there are certain things it needs to learn about itself and its environment to thrive. Considering this idea means that an individual can participate in the life and evolution of Divinity.

* * *

Space or distance creates the illusion of separateness. The stars are there, and I'm here. We're separate. But this is not the truth, merely the perception of the five senses. Whether someone is on the other side of the room or the world, one's intention or wish to connect can contact that person. Most of the time, we dismiss these occurrences unless they're profound, such as when someone we've been thinking about contacts us. This is due to what quantum physicists call Entanglement.

Esoterically speaking, we are entangled because we are all parts of the same cosmic body called the Megalocosmos. On that scale, we might all perhaps be living in the same cell of that body with a joint task to perform. All mysterious psychic phenomena, such as clairvoyance, telepathy, precognition, and others, represent an ability that can be developed because of our interconnection to all the other parts of that celestial body.

* * *

Children are born without prejudice. At a young age, when they're still open to the starry world, they know that we're all one. Some people have managed to retain that childlike sense into adulthood. Below is an excerpt from the commencement address given by the Rev. Martin Luther King Jr. in June 1965 at Oberlin College.

> Mankind is tied together; all life is interrelated, and we're caught in an inescapable network of mutuality, tied in a single garment of destiny. Whatever affects one directly, affects all indirectly. For some strange reason I can never be what I ought to be until you are what you ought to be. And you can never be what you ought to be until I am what I ought to be.

Dr. King's emotional description of Entanglement is what P. D. Ouspensky called the sixth dimension of reality, the world of all possibilities, where all points touch and affect each other in the solidity of time—an "inescapable network of mutuality."

In this sixth dimension there is no "us and them." We're all part of an unimaginably immense, interconnected, unified whole. Our wishes, thoughts, feelings, prayers, and intentions affect that entity because they are part of its makeup. We have direct control over our world if we choose to exercise that connection. We've been given a possibility to, as Mahatma Gandhi once said, "Be the change you wish to see in the world."

III.
COMMON SENSE

1: sound and prudent judgment based on a simple perception of the situation or facts.
—Merriam-Webster

A SENSE COMMON TO ALL

A. R. Orage (1873–1934) was the editor of *The New Age* magazine. He was also a student of Gurdjieff who played a crucial role in the publication of *Beelzebub's Tales to His Grandson*. He once said:

> The last degree of esoteric teaching is plain common sense. The birthright of human beings is the desire for self-consciousness, which should appear at the age of majority. At about the age of thirty there should come a sense of the world in which we live [that is] the dawning of cosmic consciousness.[48]

This "sense of the world" is common to us all, though few dare to discover their place in life and how to fulfill their purpose.

CONSCIOUSNESS

What is consciousness? The word derives from the Latin word *conscius*, meaning to know in oneself. According to *Merriam Webster*, *consciousness* is "the normal state of being able to understand what is happening around you—being aware of something within you or an external object."

Esoterically speaking, this only describes a feature of being conscious. *Consciousness* is defined as "knowing all together," and there are many levels of this state. It is not like a light switch—now I'm conscious, now I'm not. Another aspect of consciousness is that we don't possess it; we participate in it. Cosmic consciousness is at the top of the scale, and at the bottom is unconsciousness or what Gurdjieff calls *firm calm*. Our place moves along the scale as we work toward evolution or not.

Gurdjieff also proved experimentally that human beings participate on the scale of consciousness at two different levels.

> In the entirety of every man, irrespective of his heredity and education, there are formed two independent consciousnesses which in their functioning [and] their manifestations have almost nothing in common.[49]

The first he calls "pure waking consciousness:"

> The perception of all kinds of accidental or intentionally produced, mechanical impressions.[50]

In other words, it's all the opinions, judgments, estimates, views, pictures, images, and the "facts of life" stuffed into us by parents, guardians, teachers, friends, and daily life in general. On the other hand, our subconscious he defines as being:

> formed from the so to say, 'already previously formed material results' transmitted ... by heredity, which have become blended with the corresponding parts of the entirety of a man, as well as from the data arising from his intentional evoking of the associative confrontations of these 'materialized data' already in him.[51]

This definition has to be taken in small bites. The phrase, "results transmitted by heredity" means that one's subconscious is partly made of the experiences of their bloodlines. Everyone who traces their ancestry finds that they're related to an ever-increasing segment of a population, which have passed on traits to them that are still active. For example:

> An Englishman born in 1950 may be descended from perhaps a quarter of the entire population of England in Chaucer's day. Existing in him—like ancient records—he may find traces of the different aspects of his race and culture.[52]

Thus, hereditary knowledge passes down through the blood from previous generations. What Gurdjieff calls the "associative confrontations" are what we call the school of hard knocks, the accumulated experiences of daily life. "Intentionally evoking" them is the effort we make to incorporate this hard-won knowledge into our hereditary experience and being, creating the "fire is hot, don't touch" kind of understanding necessary to evolve.

The problem is that these two consciousnesses are unaware of each other, and actually, when one is awake, the other is asleep. Yet they both give us impulses, which are completely different in content from each other. From our daily knowledge, which was acquired without questioning, we get the desires of life. From our subconscious, we get understanding of ourselves and higher laws and principles. This is easier to grasp if you've had the experience of a troubling life situation resolved or your choice of direction in life clarified by a dream. This is not to say that all dreams are worth paying attention to. Most of them are mental excretions from an overfull mind.

LYING

We all hate liars, yet we all lie. And worse, we lie to ourselves. This is especially true when we call ourselves "I." *I* is that part in us that represents the Unmanifest. Children don't use this sacred word while they're still connected to the starry world. They learn it through the people around them. Up until about 18 months old, children call themselves by their name. After that, they accept what they've been told, and start using *I* to refer to themselves. Psychologists say this change comes when children realize they're a separate person with separate ideas. Esotericism teaches that it comes when the child's essential self is being overtaken by life's influences and they're starting to forget their true origins.

Though painful to watch, nothing can change this situation, and it'd be harmful to our children to try. The growth of the child's personality, though at the expense of essence, must take place. It's part of life. Children need a strong personality to make their way through the world. They will also require a rich, fully developed personality as a food source for the essence's possible later growth, like the white around a fertilized egg yolk.

When we say *I*, we're assuming a characteristic we don't possess—unified being. We are a legion of wants and desires that can't even agree with themselves most of the time—very far from directing our way through life with intention. Also, we say such things as "I am tired," or "I am hungry," or "I am cold," which is absurd. It's as if we're saying our embryonic soul is those things when it's only our physical bodies that have those sensations. Infants grasp this idea on their level of consciousness because they know there's a difference between the flood of sensations from this new world and new body, and that in them experiencing it all. Then slowly, under the heavy influences of life, those experiences are buried in them and forgotten.

Because of the widespread practice of yoga, the word *namaste* has made its way into popular culture. It can be found on candles, coffee mugs, T-shirts, phone cases, and a myriad of other items for sale. The word comes from the Vedas, the oldest religious scriptures of Hinduism, and according to their teaching, *namaste* is greeting the Divine in a fellow being. The gesture that goes with the word is of the hands together in prayer with a short bow in deference to the God particle inside the other.

Although it's difficult to grasp, *I* is not what we like about ourselves, *I* wishes for enlightenment.

SUGGESTIBILITY

In today's modern society there are people called influencers who start various trends in all different aspects of life for other people to follow. This is an ideal example of *suggestibility*, which is defined as uncritically accepting and believing what other people tell you. Gurdjieff says that it's humanity's greatest weakness. He had two driving forces behind his search for wisdom.

> To understand the exact significance and purpose of the life of man.

And:

> To discover, at all costs, some manner or means for destroying in people the predilection for suggestibility, which causes them to fall easily under the influence of mass hypnosis.[53]

He's not talking about certain other people with a "predilection for suggestibility," he's talking about *humanity*—all of us. That is a tough pill to swallow, although we can clearly see it in all the other "sheeple" around us. It's like my favorite DMV statistic: 80 percent of all drivers believe they are in the top 10 percent of good drivers.

A perusal of the headlines today will clearly show our enslavement to suggestibility. Mother Nature is literally burning up with the fever that mankind gave her, yet we're still not taking responsibility and doing everything we can to see her get well. Why not? Because of the propaganda, misinformation, and lies surrounding the issue. People don't know what to believe, so they believe nothing and do nothing. At the same time nations, states, regions, cities, towns, and individuals are warring over the planet's dwindling resources, which is another side effect of our suggestibility.

All opinions, fabrications, exaggerations, and lies exist to make us buy something, believe something, or do something. It's some people's jobs to propagate mass hypnosis in customers, clients, congregations, citizens, etc.—resulting in buying sprees, riots, wars, revolutions, and religious movements.

Early in *Beelzebub's Tales*, Gurdjieff declares that all our knowledge is from suggestibility. Everything we know is because someone told us, without any verification on our part. This is primarily the result of a mechanism that makes us believe what we hear if it's repeated often or comes from someone, we think we can trust. This is another consequence of the properties of the organ Kundabuffer.

Joseph Goebbels, the minister of propaganda for the Nazi regime's rise to power in the 1930s, understood this idea. He said that if you repeat a lie often enough it becomes the truth.

> It does not require much self-observation to notice how one is extraordinarily suggestible all day long to what one hears or reads or sees or is told. You listen to a speech that you think is very powerful and then you listen to an opposite speech and you think that is very powerful. All advertising, propaganda [slogans and marketing] are based on the suggestibility of a man or a woman. This suggestibility in ourselves is one of our greatest weaknesses and leads to imitation.[54]

This was written in the early 1950s, and our situation has worsened exponentially. There were no cell phones or personal computers then—devices that continuously suggest to us things to like, not like, buy, or boycott, including political, religious, and social positions. According to a June 30, 2023, article by Steven Zauderer written on behalf of Cross River Therapy, the average person spends almost seven hours a day on a screen connected to the internet. That's 40 percent of their waking hours. What are your thoughts on where this will lead, regarding people's actual participation in their lives?

Socrates said, "To know yourself, think for yourself."

LOSING SELF-IMPORTANCE

At the end of Castaneda's apprenticeship to don Juan, he was given the "sorcerer's explanation"[55] and sent into the world, his teacher's task of passing on the knowledge complete. One of don Juan's profound lessons was on Losing Self-Importance.

> As long as you feel that you are the most important thing in the world, you cannot appreciate the world around you. You are like a horse with blinders; all you see is yourself apart from everything else.[56]

Self-importance is an exaggerated opinion of one's value or importance—the attribute of being overly vain. If we conduct an honest appraisal, we may see that our feelings of self-worth all too often rest on what others think of us because it inflates or deflates our self-importance. Hence our slavish reliance on the opinion of others. Yet, we can loosen this tyrant's grip on us.

The antonym of *self-importance* is *humility*—though this noble word has accumulated pejorative connotations such as unassertiveness, diffidence, and lacking pride. These are not traits of those paragons of humility: Jesus Christ, Mother Teresa, and Mahatma Gandhi. Humility is the starting point for reordering one's life from the top down from our highest and finest wishes. It's humbling to realize that I've yet done little to make myself useful or valuable in the cosmic scheme of things. Usually, I've been distracted by the outer and inner worlds, both filled with petty tyrants trying to get their own way. Be it cause or effect, this "me, me, me first" attitude is in sync with the dark times we live in. But there is a choice.

Dante Alighieri (1265–1321) was an Italian poet who wrote the epic narrative poem, *The Divine Comedy*, on his concepts of Heaven, Hell, and Purgatory. He placed the feature of self-importance in a special spot in Hell. These sinners are sitting around a grand banquet table laden with food and drink. Their punishment is to have their arms fixed straight out in front of them so they can neither bend at the elbow or wrist to bring food to their mouths. They could turn to their neighbors and feed each other, but the weight of their sin will not let them see another eat first. So, every night, with delectable food within reach, these wretches starve to death.

Self-importance makes us feel apart from the world. When its grip loosens on our hearts, we experience the fear of becoming unimportant. Yet mysteriously, when we are less self-important, we are more valuable to Creation and the Creator.

EVERY STICK ALWAYS HAS TWO ENDS

This simple saying makes us think, "Why, of course. That makes sense." Yet the meaning of this adage goes deeper than what's perceived at first glance. The poor state of our world reflects the lack of understanding of the idea contained in this expression, meaning that every action always has a positive and negative consequence.

> Every cause occurring in the life of a man, from whatever phenomenon it arises . . . is obligatorily molded also into two quite opposite effects, as for instance: if 'something' obtained from two different causes engenders light, then it must inevitably engender a phenomenon opposite to it, that is to say darkness . . .[57]

In other words, taking the easy way or the clean end of the stick on any task leaves the problematic or dirty side for another. In reverse, when we intentionally take the more difficult end and do the extra work required, we give a straightforward, simpler task to the other. Gurdjieff called this "external consideration." Simply put, if I take the extra time and effort to put my refuse out neatly and compactly, it makes the job easier for the person picking it up.

It isn't a world-shattering change to ensure that my garbage doesn't blow all over the place, making a mess for others to clean. Doing a neat, thorough job adds beauty and order to the world and lessens a fellow human being's burden, which eases the suffering of the Divine.

> And the King shall answer and say unto them, Verily I say unto you, Inasmuch as ye have done it unto one of the least of these my brethren, ye have done it unto me.[58]

Children must be shown early in life that actions have both of these consequences. A parent or guardian using extra patience and understanding will positively instill this idea in a child—like gently, yet insistently, seeing to it that they do their assigned homework properly. Why is this taking the dirty end of the stick? It can be exasperating getting a child to do their work (not unlike getting us to do ours when we don't want to). But making that extra effort helps a child develop a positive work ethic and become a useful, productive member of the household and society.

On the other hand, letting a child do it "their own way," gives them the dirty end of the stick because without our guidance and discipline most children will fail in life.

THREE INJUNCTIONS

In chapter one of *Beelzebub's Tales*, Gurdjieff offers three injunctions for someone serious about obtaining enlightenment.

IN LIFE, NEVER DO AS OTHERS DO:
This idea comes from Gnosticism, which developed over a millennium ago among early Christian and Jewish sects. Gnostics emphasized spiritual knowledge over strict orthodox tradition. The early Catholic hierarchy saw them as a threat to the "true faith," declared their belief heresy, and excommunicated or killed their followers. Luckily, their teaching was rediscovered in 1947 as part of the Dead Sea Scroll find—gospels that were composed during Jesus Christ's lifetime. One purportedly direct quote is "Follow me, and you shall lose me. Follow yourselves, and you shall find both me and yourselves."[59]

According to Joseph Campbell, this is the call to the Left-Hand path. Campbell gives the Knights of the Round Table as another example of the call. In one story of this esoteric tale told by traveling bards in medieval times, King Arthur is challenging his knights to quest for the Holy Grail:

> And they decided to do so, but they thought it would be a disgrace to go forth in a group. Each entered the forest at a place that he had chosen where it was darkest and there was no way or path. That is to say each must find his own path.[60]

Spiritual evolution cannot be gained by following another on their path because the process is individual. You can follow the signs left by others on the way, but the choice of which way to go remains yours.

VERIFY EVERY SUSPICIOUS "ACTUAL FACT":
One of Gurdjieff's tales from his childhood is about a time another "ragamuffin of a boy" knocked his tooth out.

> This strange tooth had seven roots and at the end of each root, there stood out in relief a drop of blood, and through each separate drop, there shone clearly and definitely one of the seven aspects of the manifestation of the white ray.[61]

When he showed this amazing tooth to a barber/surgeon, the local expert on such things, he was told it wasn't special, "just a wisdom tooth: everybody had them." Nothing special is life's all-too-frequent response to the miraculous, and why authority must be questioned. It's a dangerous assumption that being in charge equals understanding.

Luckily for Gurdjieff, the cavity never healed correctly, and it always

> had the property of arousing an interest in, and a tendency to seek out the causes of the arising of every suspicious 'actual fact.'[62]

It's easy to take "trusted experts" at their word, especially ones that strike a chord with us. Yet everyone's fallible. Esotericism teaches us to verify everything, in particular what a teacher says. Doing your own due diligence is taking responsibility for your own choices, your life, and your evolution.

WHEN YOU GO ON A SPREE, GO WHOLE HOG, INCLUDING THE POSTAGE:
This "all universal principle of living" is practically self-explanatory. If you're making a wish, don't scrimp—go all the way and willingly pay any extra unforeseen cost to attain your aim. It will prepare you for those unexpected circumstances you encounter and help you stay positive when they arise. People's aims usually fail because they give up five minutes too soon, cut corners, or refuse to pay some unexpected charge or make some necessary extra effort.

Regarding this idea of going all the way, don Juan told Castaneda that:

> When a man decides to do something, he must go all the way . . . but he must take responsibility for what he does. No matter what he does, he must know first why he is doing it, and then he must proceed with his actions without having doubts or remorse about them.[63]

This includes a willingness to pay in full up front in order to accomplish an aim. Not paying comes from thinking there's time to look for a cheaper and easier way.

QUESTION EVERYTHING

This is not a catch phrase but a mandate for a truth-seeker. As Socrates said, "The unexamined life is not worth living." If we never questioned our beliefs, why do we believe them? Am I satisfied to live an imaginary life full of fictional convictions, or do I need to know and understand things for myself?

We accept many tales as true because we hear them when we're young, and they're repeated often by the people around us. And when we do ask questions, even from the best intentions possible, adults usually squash the impulse: "Stop with all the questions! You're driving me nuts." (Oft times we even say this to ourselves.)

But we shouldn't stop, and nothing should be off-limits to our investigations. Take the biblical story of Adam and Eve from the book of Genesis—book one of the Hebrew Bible, and book one of the Christian Old Testament. For Judeo-Christians, this is the tale of humanity's beginning on Earth. It's also the first story of good and evil. The short oral version of the story is well-known; reading the text, however, there seems to be sections that have an underlying agenda not from the heavens.

The book of Genesis is thought to have been written some thirty-five hundred years ago. Historically, it was a time of war for the Israelites, who were fighting to create a homeland. Men ruled the country, their household, and their wives—and religion ruled men. It's still much the same today in the Middle East.

Some religious scholars believe God dictated the book of Genesis to Moses. Others believe it's a combination of Moses' teachings, already existing religious texts, and older esoteric manuscripts that were edited together for flow and continuity, and in places "fitted" into the current religious and political thinking. If the second scenario is a more accurate picture of events, then the writing should reflect dissimilar styles and changes in voice and tone, as different writers write differently. Interestingly, there are parts of the book of Genesis that have that feel, as though they're the result of numerous roundtable discussions by religious authorities, compiling an approved version of a Creation story.

One section that possibly resulted from a conference is just after God created man:

> The Lord God said, It is not good that the man should be alone . . . and He took one of his ribs, and closed up the flesh; . . . and the rib, which the Lord God had taken from man, made He a woman . . .[64]

Now, except for the Gods and Goddesses of ancient world religions (like Athena being born from the head of Zeus), there is no creature in the cosmos that came into existence differently from its mate, because that would make them a different species. What this story is saying about the relationship of Eve to Adam sounds suspect, like Church doctrine has slipped into a real idea.

Later in the tale, Eve is tempted by Satan embodied as a serpent to eat the fruit of the knowledge of good and evil. Eve yields to temptation and then tempts Adam, who also succumbs and eats the fruit. When the Lord finds out, He expels them from the Garden of Eden, where they've so far enjoyed a life free from toil, worry, and pain. Their expulsion bestowed on humanity all the ills that plague us today, and women have taken the blame ever since.

Here lies the rub—not yet possessing the knowledge of good and evil, Adam and Eve couldn't choose to be obedient or disobedient. They didn't understand subterfuge. They were in the world as babies, experiencing it for the first time. The story clearly says that only after eating the fruit did they know what they'd done and were ashamed. Does it feel right and just that the Eternal, All-knowing, All-loving Creator of the Megalocosmos would banish Its finest creation from sight and force them into a life of pain and hard labor for one childhood transgression? There must be something else going on.

The biblical account of Adam and Eve also raises many theological questions. Wasn't planting the tree in the middle of the Garden already a temptation? Why didn't the Lord want Adam and Eve to know the difference between good and evil? Why did God lie to Adam about dying if he ate the fruit? Why is the serpent the one telling the truth? And, the most troubling question: why is the tone so different here from the Creation story that preceded it?

> So, God created man in His own image, in the image of God created He him: male and female created He them.[65]

It's possible that this section of the text is from a much older esoteric work. If we boldly change a word in the above quote (which may have been badly translated to begin with), it would read, "created *mankind* in His own image." The grammar makes more sense, as does the impossible number of offspring supposedly from one set of parents, all questions of inbreeding aside. What if Adam and Eve represent the first *peoples* to be seeded on Earth? They'd be the Adam Kadmon of the Hebrew Kabbalah—mankind's past, present, and future; the essence of humanity created in the image and likeness of the Lord God;

created to occupy and tend to the earth. In other words, the *idea of Mankind* was created.

Another place where the scribes were possibly hard at work is in this story of the creation of Woman.

> And the rib, which the Lord God had taken from the man, made He a woman and brought her unto the man. And Adam said, this is now bone of my bones, and flesh of my flesh: she shall be called Woman, because she was taken out of Man.[66]

This account feels like a continuation of Adam naming Earth's creatures over whom he has dominion. The miraculous has been debased to a teaching about Woman's *place* in the world, ignoring their equal role in creation (the men with wombs) solely to legitimize their repression.

Whether these ideas strike you as true or false, good or bad, right or wrong, thought-provoking or blasphemous—discussion is the point. This essay is an examination of preconceived notions, especially regarding religious ideas about the purpose of life and the position we occupy in the created universe.

Today's world is in the grip of zealots from every major religion. They believe fanatically in their cause and rhetoric to the exclusion of all other thoughts, and they're willing to destroy the entire world to see their agendas accomplished. Apparently, they've never heard the Prophet Muhammad's teaching of Allah's all-forgiving and all-merciful love or Christ's words about loving your enemies.

We all have these voices of violence and hatred in us. They scream to have their way and are willing to take us down to get it. One way to silence them is to starve them to death by depriving them of the energy of our attention. The energy saved then can be more profitably given over to finer impulses.

SEEING REALITY

R OY G. BIV is an age-old acronym used to remember the colors of the visible light spectrum: red, orange, yellow, green, blue, indigo, and violet. Recently, there's been a movement to eliminate indigo from the rainbow because the human eye does not readily see hues in the wavelengths between blue and violet.

> Modern physics generally accepts a six-color spectrum. Indigo is omitted because few people can differentiate the wavelengths well enough to see it as a separate color.[67]

Indigo still exists in nature, but people are losing the ability to see the color distinctly. Typically, we believe that progress is ongoing, and we're better off than those savages who came before us, but our forbearers saw the color in the rainbow, which makes this a documented case for the diminishment of mankind's ability to see reality—a bitter pill to swallow.

The foundations of Western science were set in ancient Greece by Natural Philosophers observing their surroundings and formulating logical reasons for what they saw. One of these early scientists, Democritus (460–370 BCE), while contemplating the coast of the Aegean Sea, noted that the beach resulted from endless grains of sand. Each grain was tiny and insignificant, yet together, they formed the expansive beaches. He extrapolated that all matter is similarly composed of minuscule indivisible pieces, which he called *atoma*.

In this context, *indivisible* means that the particle is the tiniest bit of a substance that still retains the whole's physical, psychic, and cosmic properties in the same proportions. Atoma come in all shapes and sizes. Some, like an atoma of bread, are large enough to see with the naked eye. An atoma of ocean tastes like the ocean, and multiplying it by an astronomical number creates a large body of salty water that can support life.

Indivisible also means that further reduction changes the atoma into something else. For instance, the separated atoms of seawater—oxygen, hydrogen, salt, etc.—cannot support life by themselves. They are not atomas of an ocean. Yet modern science continues to investigate the world by dissection: looking at smaller and smaller pieces in the hopes of seeing the whole.

Ironically, that dogged persistence took a particular study under the influence of the esoteric truism, "Any idea followed to the end will lead to enlightenment." Scientists studying tiny pieces of matter moving at impossible speeds in the briefest periods of time discovered that the universe is a giant, organic, unified, living whole. That's quantum physics talking, not mysticism, religion, or philosophy.

One's worldview determines how they see reality. If you look at life as a complex clockwork, like the nihilistic philosophy of Mechanism—the theory that physical causes can explain natural phenomena—that makes you one of numerous cogs in a series of unconnected machines. The gears around you make your decisions, and you cannot change anything. If you believe the Universe is a living, breathing being, then one's possibilities are almost limitless.

One opportunity is an increase in the ability to see reality—to see what is. The first step is to admit that we don't. But then we often encounter an obstacle encapsulated in the two words, "I know," which stops wondering and investigation. Our minds store all our beliefs, yet most of what we fill them with is what we've been told with little investigation and verification.

Some things have to be taken on faith, but people can be mentally lazy. Despite appearances to the contrary, we want to be told what to think rather than discover things for ourselves. First of all, it's a lot of work. And something in us wants someone else to take responsibility for our choices. We think it's better than to risk the consequences of being wrong.

The Megalocosmos came into existence by Divine impulse, and was made manifest through Divine laws. Humanity is part of that impulse, seeded on Earth in the hopes that some of us will evolve into friends and helpmates for Divinity. According to Gurdjieff, the number of celestial movements requires there be "all quarters maintainers" to coordinate them. Though primarily an archangel's work, there are job openings at every level of the Megalocosmos.

The wish to be useful is part of being human, which includes parenting, child and elder care, volunteering, teaching, coaching, nursing, and a myriad of other worthy causes. Yet do we ever wonder if Divinity needs anything from us? Dare we see reality from that lofty a place where we can ask, "Lord, what can I do for You today?" and then wait for an answer? We may scoff at this idea, but then why were we created?

> And the Lord God took the man, and put him into the Garden of Eden to dress it and to keep it.[68]

Doesn't this imply that there's work to be done, and the Lord created human beings to help with the project?

SAFEGUARDING ALARM CLOCKS

Most people have a love-hate relationship with their alarm clocks. Although they're indispensable in helping us keep our appointments, fulfilling that function can earn them anything from verbal abuse to physical harm. This is especially true when asking friends to remind us of our wishes, and help keep us awake to them like helping us stay on a diet or quit smoking. Their help can often produce very negative consequences—for them.

Psychological alarm clocks only benefit that part of us that wishes to evolve. The other parts—I daresay the larger piece of us—is content with the status quo, preferring to continue sleeping peacefully. An alarm clock's survival depends on which way we throw our weight when we hear it sounding off.

We have similar internal alarms, helping to keep us awake to our wishes and dreams, and warning us when we stray from our path. Sadly, they often suffer the same fate as others of their kind. We need to be on guard against what's within us that wants us to fail, undermines us, and even plots to do us harm. Are you familiar with the voice inside that always recalls past mistakes, and tells you that you're bad or worthless because of them?

In *Beelzebub's Tales*, Gurdjieff gives an example of how to shield yourself from these negative voices in his story about the Karapet of Tiflis. In deference to this Karapet's advanced age and the many years of his dedicated service to the Tiflis Railroad, he was relieved of heavier duties and assigned the task of releasing steam into a loud whistle every morning, calling all the railroad employees to work. During the first week of performing his new duty, the Karapet felt "vaguely ill at ease," and this condition persisted, lasting six months. He spent much of that time trying to understand what was happening to him, and finally found the reason for the maleficent feelings he was having.

> [I] accidentally and suddenly understood why I experienced this uneasiness... everyone awakened by the noise I make with the steam whistle, which disturbs his sweet morning slumbers, must, without doubt, curse me 'by everything under the sun,'... and thanks to this, there must of course certainly flow towards my person from all directions, vibrations of all kinds of malice.[69]

Historical notes: since 1936 the city of Tiflis has been called Tbilisi, and it's the capital of Georgia at the crossroads of Western Asia and Eastern Europe. *Karapet* is an old Armenian word for *precursor*, someone who comes before another. There is a church in Tbilisi called Saint Karapet, which is dedicated to the Christian saint, John the Baptist, the precursor of the Christ. It's not a stretch to think of John the Baptist's role in the Bible as an alarm clock. Traditionally, he called people to wake up and prepare because the Christ was coming. Historically, he also tried to awaken King Herod to his crimes against the people of Judea, and was summarily executed for it—the sad fate of many alarm clocks.

The Karapet of Tiflis discovered a way to defend against the negativity hurled his way in the mornings. His investigations led him to conclude that if he cursed "beforehand all those to whom [this] service for the benefit of certain among them [was] disturbing,"[70] then the negativity aimed at him wouldn't have any effect. And indeed, that's what happened. Every morning, before he pulled the rope to release the steam into the whistle, he cursed all the townsfolk in all four directions, creating a shield against the voices wishing him harm that came at him afterward.

We can use the same method for the same protection. Out of earshot of others, loudly curse everyone and anyone that could possibly be sending negative vibrations your way: family, friends, workmates, neighbors, newspapers, internet, TV, radio or strangers. And don't be polite about it—curse them with the vilest names you know, wishing them misfortune in abundance. Curse them first, and you may feel a curious relief throughout the rest of your day. Repeat as often as needed.

Note: fire plugs and fence posts make good listeners.

THE DISEASE OF MAÑANA

According to Gurdjieff, procrastination is not the same as the disease Mañana because it's not just putting things off. One aspect of this disease is being satisfied with the imagination of the amount and quality of work we will do—tomorrow. As Dr, Maurice Nicoll (1884–1953), a Scottish psychiatrist and close student of Ouspensky, says,

> Change of being begins with changing your reactions to actual incidents of the day. This is the beginning of taking your life in a real and practical sense in a new way. If you behave in the same way every day to the same recurring events of the day, how can you believe you can change?[71]

One thing making us susceptible to the disease of Mañana is the fear of failure. Another thing is the fear of success. In other words, it's the fear of the unknown and the consequences it might bring. But what if you fail? Did you make so enormous a gamble that the life and health of yourself and others are in jeopardy? Is there no work-around? What if you succeed? What changes will you have to make in your life? Are you willing to change? These are all troubling questions for that part of us wanting a peaceful, quiet, and consistently uneventful life.

Michelangelo (1475–1564), one of the master artists of the Italian High Renaissance, once said,

The greater danger for most of us lies not in setting our aim too high and falling short, but in setting our aim too low and achieving our mark.

If you wish to spiritually develop, the time is now. Every tomorrow too soon becomes yesterday, and before we realize it, we no longer have the energy to change. Every process has a time limit. There is a saying from the ancient Hebrew rabbinical text called the Talmud, that roughly translates to,

If not me, who? If not now, when?[72]

You may have also heard the maxim, *Strike while the iron is hot*. This comes from the blacksmith trade. They knew that after the iron was heated, there was only a short time it could be worked before it cooled off and had to be reheated. Beating on cold steel ruins it. The problem for us is that in regards to our spiritual development, we will eventually run out of time and energy to reheat ourselves.

CHOOSING YOUR THOUGHTS

Our ability to discern truth from falsehood is battered daily by life's deceit, duplicity, and hypocrisy. Each waking moment, we're bombarded by outrageous advertising claims, pompous political rhetoric, lies, foreboding religious oratory, disinformation, pretense, scams—the list goes on and on. This onslaught leaves us stunned, jaded, and cynical.

Part of the problem is the feature of our lower natures that believes we can trust something because we've seen it in print or some digital form. This is the power and the problem of our age. The internet—filled by sound bites, videos, memes, and whatnot—provides a nonstop flow of opinions from anyone with a computer and an agenda. These loud, strident voices, typically accompanied by mean-spirited feelings and wild, shameless antics capture our attention. This is suggestibility.

In plain English, we don't think for ourselves. We absorb the most prevalent theories of the time, or are in strict opposition to them. We follow influencers (I still laugh) selling every kind of theory and philosophy of how to look, like, and live. Yet today's gestalt can be summed up by the phrase, "Hooray for me and to hell with everybody else." This inner attitude feeds the lowest level in us and fragments society into smaller and more zealous groups. This is easily verified by a brief scan of today's headlines, which all depict "us versus them" situations. The more vitriolic voices are the same as those heard during the Dark Ages, a time when "might made right," and the powerful ran roughshod over the weak, who were considered no more than personal property or part of the landscape.

The first Arthurian legend dates back to the early ninth century, 350 years after the Western Roman Empire's collapse. The times were brutal and unforgiving, and the population had been decimated by war and disease. Rome had gone from a million residents down to 30,000, with less than half of all children surviving past early childhood. Yet a certain number of people's faith, hope, love, and prayer brought the idea of King Arthur and his knights into the world, which restored goodness, justice, and decency in mankind's heart. (An example of conscious beings changing the world.)

Today, negativity is a rewardable trait for various types of celebrities and politicians. They spew their venom without regard for any other's welfare, making huge fortunes in the process. Part of the Good Word Jesus Christ brought to the world is that we don't have to be at the mercy of voices outside or inside of us.

> Not that which goeth into the mouth defileth a man; but that which cometh out of the mouth, this defileth a man.[73]

Dr. Nicoll wrote a series of books titled, *Psychological Commentaries on the Teaching of Gurdjieff and Ouspensky*. He interprets the above quote as:

> The thought that enters the mind is what goes *into a man*. What he thinks and does from this thought is what comes *out of him*.[74]

In other words, thoughts enter us from the outside. They are not ours, and we don't have to claim them or even pay attention to them. We can choose which thoughts to listen to and act on. Those we chose to disregard will eventually continue on their way back out of us. As they pass through, some of them might try to out-shout all the others to claim our attention, but a higher volume does not obligate us to listen to them.

Party lines are typically adhered to because of the concern for what others will think of us, and of course, we don't want to stand out from our fellows in the wrong way. The problem is that everyone feels the same way, and they're all waiting to see what the leadership and the other members will do. This is one of the reasons why group decisions take so long to make.

On the other hand, everything is an open topic today. From this perspective, the internet makes it easier to investigate false ideas and claims, which will help us decide which thoughts are worth thinking. However, we must perform due diligence and verify the so-called facts for ourselves to our own satisfaction. Working toward evolution is just that—work. It is impossible to spiritually grow by following the pack. That's why it's called individual evolution—it is an individual effort.

If the epitome of a man's or woman's spiritual journey is to become a brain cell in the mind of God, there can be no copies. It's like the story of the religious man who upon his death stood at the pearly gates. St. Peter asked him what he did with his life to deserve entrance into Heaven, and he replies with humble pride that he strived his whole life to be like Moses. The response is stunning because St. Peter turned him away, saying, "We already have a Moses."

KEEP YOUR BRAINS CLEAN

Esotericism teaches that we are designed with multiple brains or centers to control our planetary body's functions. The planetary body is not just our flesh-and-bone package—it's also our psychic, spiritual, and cosmic container. Two of these centers are the thinking brain and the feeling brain—one is in our head, and the other is centered close to our hearts in the solar plexus.

Everyone is familiar with the thinking brain's lower functions: comparison, calculation, conclusion, etc. This part is filled with yes/no questions, small plans, quantities, sums, and judgments. Yet the thinking brain also has a higher part that is fully operational yet untapped. This higher intellectual function connects us to higher worlds, and it's interesting to note that access to this higher part is through our higher emotional brain.

The language of the intellectual brain is thoughts, phrases, and words. Pictures, symbols, and expressions are the language of the emotional brain. That is one of the difficulties that "feeling" people and "thinking" people have in communicating: they speak different languages. This same situation happens inside with our brains; one doesn't understand the other.

Companies direct their advertising at our emotional brains because they don't weigh and decide, they like and dislike. Here, the details don't matter. It's the polished image that leads us to make costly purchases or to believe certain things. (Remember my "show" bike.) That's one of the reasons sex sells so well. It gives us a positive emotional charge, and we feel alive without much effort on our part. That titillation draws us to what's advertised. The emotional brain is easily led by someone who learns which buttons to push. That's why there are crimes of passion.

News broadcasts are similarly directed at our emotional centers, where images and sounds, especially the commentator's tone and tenor, are trying to affect how we'll feel and react. One way to verify this is to listen to how a person speaks. Are they showing you the emotions they hope to elicit? Try turning the sound off on a video broadcast or commercial to see if the effect is different with just the pictures. At a guess, it's less than half as effective capturing your attention. It works the same with the sound on and the picture off, though sounds are more effective at grabbing our attention.

All this emotional manipulation has a hidden spiritual cost, yet we can't become hermits. We have to interact with the world in which we live. So, can we keep our brains clean without cutting ourselves off from society? The first step is to confirm that this is a type of pollution in your life. Did you notice a change with the sound off? Have you noticed other instances where life is trying to steal your energy, time, and money?

If you wake up to news broadcasts and the accompanying advertising, you're unnecessarily starting your day under negative influences. Try waking up to music that inspires you. It's also helpful to wait an hour after rising before diving into the day's events. And when you do turn something on—news, emails, messages, texts, or whatever—remember it's an influence. Try not to drown in it. Come up for air now and again—and give yourself higher and finer thoughts and feelings.

We're inundated at every turn with people trying to get us to do one thing or another. Remember: what you see or hear is not you. It's an attempt by a possibly nefarious source to make as many people as possible feel a certain way. If you can begin to grasp the level of suggestibility involved in daily life, you'll become less susceptible to its influence.

As Socrates said, "To find yourself, think for yourself."

REQUESTING YOUR WORLD

The science of quantum physics has proven that human intention affects the apparent randomness of the Universe. In other words, the life we see all around us every day has been partially created by our intentions. This is because the tiniest bits of matter yet discovered at the foundation of the created world exhibit properties of both waves *and* particles. These scientists showed that when you're observing matter, they're particles of experience. When you're not looking, they're waves of possibilities.

Esoterically this means that before we decide on an interpretation of an experience, numerous possibilities exist. Yet how we typically feel and think about the world and how we expect to see it every day is how it's presented to us. In other words, we create the world we live in because we've decided how things are in that world. However, when we understand that all possibilities exist until we fix them in place, we can choose the outcome of almost every situation. This is at the heart of the esoteric idea that the universe is response to request.

"But," you say, "*I'm* not living the life I want. If this idea is true, why am I not getting what I'm asking for?" This idea says that you *are* living the life you've asked for, you're just unaware that you've asked for it. For example, someone says, "I wish to be happy." No sooner are the words out of their mouth than they get into an argument with some "idiot" who didn't know one end of a stick from another.

A deeper examination of that person's intentions as they made the wish to be happy may reveal that in that moment, a part of them was more concerned with being right. (This is all too often the case with human beings.) The part wishing to be right was the loudest, shouting its request to the universe. So, they're provided with an opportunity to prove to themselves at least that they were right, believing the other person was a fool, even if that wasn't objectively true.

It may be difficult to comprehend, but our inner state is in control of our outer life. Dale Carnegie (1888–1955), the author of *How to Win Friends and Influence People*, taught that it's possible to alter people's behavior by altering one's behavior toward them.

For example, recently, I had a poor attitude toward the owner of a store I frequent. I didn't know him personally, but he always rubbed me the wrong way. After one shopping trip, I returned home to discover he'd shorted my order. I was angry because I knew it was just like him to do such a thing to me. I even debated never going back the store again, but I enjoyed his products. I decided to give the owner the benefit of the doubt and consider it an honest mistake. The next time I went there with no animosity toward him, and I pleasantly said good morning, I was shocked when he greeted me like an old friend and filled my order cheerfully and carefully.

The first step to getting what you want from life is to be the one making the request. In order to do that, you have to know who in you is currently asking. In my case, it was old negative habits of annoyance and persecution accompanied by the thought, "Don't you know who I am?" Yet if I wanted their product and a pleasant experience shopping there, I had to change.

To formulate an aim for how you wish to be treated by life takes time and effort. One obstacle in doing this is our poor attention span. The average person loses their attention every six to seven seconds per minute. If you add up all the other claims on that minute—family, work, friends, relatives, community, church, clubs, etc.—it leaves little time to formulate a real request, which has to be clear and specific in order to be heard.

Another obstacle to making a real request is that most people don't know or believe that they can affect their reality in a consistent, substantial way. Esotericism teaches that the life we yearn for is waiting just above us. We only need to step up into it. The human brain, our interpreter of reality, consists of billions of nerve cells, sending and receiving millions of messages to and from all parts of the body, telling us what's real. The marvel in this design is that the individual brain cells don't touch. They're "connected in a neural net," transferring messages by passing energy through the void, jumping the gaps between cells. The lack of hard-wiring allows for change, meaning that by the grace of God, we're designed to live the life we wish for.

IV.
ESOTERIC CHRISTIANITY

"Esoteric Christianity refers to the study of the occult or mystic esoteric knowledge related to the inner teachings of Christianity. The term is generally associated with the Essenes and later the Rosicrucians. In esoteric Christianity, the religion of the Christ is taught as a mystery religion."

—Wikipedia

ESOTERICISM

The dictionary defines *esoteric* as intended for or likely to be understood by only a small number of people with a specialized knowledge or interest. As was said, there are many levels of the universe and of the people that inhabit it. Those seeking out the Left-Hand path are searching for the truth that is often hidden in the facts of life.

> And the disciples came, and said unto him, Why speakest thou unto them in parables? [Jesus] answered and said unto them, Because it is given unto you to know the mysteries of the kingdom of heaven, but to them it is not given. (Matthew 13: 10–11, KJV)

GOD'S BIG TOE (THEORY OF EVERYTHING)

One of quantum physics' recent mind-bending discoveries is that the universe is actually a highly interconnected organism that extends infinitely through time and space. Early in my parochial school years I learned that atoms, with their sun-like nucleus and planet-like electrons orbiting them, are similar in construction to our solar system. Strangely, the ratios of distance and size also seemed related. One keen wit in my class concluded that our entire solar system could merely be an atom of God's big toe. Connecting the dots between science and religion, this is not such a far-fetched idea.

In Rodney Collin's book, *The Theory of Celestial Influence*, he describes the Megalocosmos as having a spherical structure. On one side is an *absolute* white-hot pole, and on the opposite side is an *absolute* dark-cold pole. At these poles, radiation and mass

> become entirely separated, the South pole representing . . . pure radiation and the North pole pure mass. Within this sphere are an infinite number of physical conditions, an infinite number of relations to either pole, separated by definite periods [of time].[75]

This is the Law of Three at the highest level, sending the creative impulse out from its active pole into its receptive pole, generating galaxies, stars, planets, moons, and every being on them. Accordingly, the Megalocosmos is the physical body of the Unmanifest Creator. In other words, His body is His dwelling place as our planetary body is the dwelling place of our unmanifest spirit. *As above, so below.*

Modern science studies physical bodies, but it knows little or nothing of the animating force in them because they can't quantify it. That part of the created world is conveniently left out of modern scientific examination. Yet we can see the Divine manifesting all around us—just not with our cellular eyes alone. Our mind's eye sees the organization in the world, and our heart feels the pulse of life in everything. If you need proof, watch a newborn as they look at the world for the first time. If the Divine is in anything, It's in everything.

René Descartes (1596–1650), the sixteenth century French mathematician-philosopher, unfortunately gave up trying to bridge the gap between science and religion, and instead came up with the idea of Dualism, separating the seen and the unseen. He assigned the seen to science and the unseen to religion, and that was that. Sadly, this partial and corrupted view of reality wormed its way into modern thinking to denigrate women and men down to tiny parts in a giant machine governed by immutable laws. From this worldview sprang the perverse idea of people as human resources, no more than interchangeable parts on a shelf.

It takes an extra effort, especially these days, to see the good or the Divine at work in the world, but it is possible. There are unexplained things that pique our curiosity. If we don't assume there must be a modern scientific answer, we give ourselves space to wonder. And if your world is rocked, there's no need to steady it quickly. Agitation is a necessary component of evolution.

Trying to see the world through a newborn's eyes can get us agitated. As adults, we see trees as beautiful because we're sure they're trees, and of course, we know what trees are. But what if we understood that what we knew as "tree" was only a tiny fraction of what it truly was? Suppose what we saw as "tree" was a being in a frozen moment of its fifth dimension? Its roots reach into the earth, transforming soil and water to food and providing a means of communicating with its neighbors. What if we sensed the breath passing in and out of its leaves while the sap circulating inside its trunk was similar to the blood in our veins? Suppose we felt the vibrations it was transforming from the Earth and its atmosphere into food it sent back out into the world.

If we forget that we already know everything about life, there's a chance to rekindle our childlike wonder and see a brand-new world.

RELIGION

This is a difficult subject to discuss because people have a vested interest in their perspective. We're indoctrinated into the religion or nonreligion we grew up with, switched over to, or left. Religion as it's presented requires no thought. As a matter of fact, thinking for oneself is frowned upon in every major religion. There are only tenants of belief to be memorized and followed in order to be a good Christian, Muslim, Buddhist, or whatever.

Religious training usually begins at a very young age and leaves a lasting feeling that questioning anything is going against God. This pernicious fallacy is deeply rooted in our psychology. For instance, what if the story of Judas is misunderstood, and he's really a hero of the Christian faith? We'll never know. We're not allowed to ask this question because it's still considered a heretical teaching by the Catholic Church.

Organized religion wants their followers to believe as Joseph Campbell said, "only they have the goods, so to speak." There is no true search for enlightenment in any organized religion, as proved by the catastrophic religious wars that continue to be fought up to this day. Religion more than any other influence has also been at the center of the justification for men controlling women in thought, word, and deed.

Who are these fathers of the church, the scribes and clerics that believe only *they* have interpreted holy ideas the correct way? How did Christ's teaching of love turn into the persecution, torture, and killing of nonbelievers? The Indigenous American genocide is traceable back to elders of the various

Christian sects who declared all other religions devil worship, granting their followers the right to purge the heathens from the Earth. This is happening even today as fanatics strive to convert the world to their faith, or destroy it in the attempt. Concurrently, this leads to further subjugation of women and exploding child abuse and mortality rates.

In *Beelzebub's Tales*, we're repeatedly enjoined to widen our horizon and raise our perception. This means to question the so-called "facts" our religions present us with. How can it be wrong to question in the quest for the Divine? Only those with something personal to lose—power, riches, comfort—refuse to allow people's minds to open. All Messengers from Above—Christ, Buddha, Muhammad, Moses, and many others—were sent here to show us how to rid ourselves of the consequences of the organ Kundabuffer and find our way back to the starry world, not start a religion. Their followers misunderstood the message.

We all want to believe that *our* religious teachings come directly from God. However, it takes only a cursory study of any religious doctrine or dogma to see that almost all of it comes from man's misinterpretation of the teachings of a Divine messenger. All of today's major religions have come to us passed down from various councils, attempting to work higher ideas to their own purposes. The gospels, for instance, were written hundreds of years after Christ lived. The first book of the Bible, the book of Moses was written long after his passing. Even the Holy Koran was dictated to scribes who compiled what they heard long after the profit Muhammad's death.

Almost all the holy texts we have were written by men trying to codify higher ideas for the masses. It's tough to swallow the idea that religions support one political/social point of view or another. This does not mean that there's no holy truth or goodness in religion. But you can only see that if you stay critical in your thinking. Messengers were sent from above to show people how to find the way back to Heaven through their own efforts. Divinity is not looking for blind followers but for individual women and men wishing to become helpmates.

WHAT THE DEVIL?

A Devil is a God who has not been recognized. [That is to say,] a disregarded Deity becomes a devil, so nature becomes feared.[76]

From earliest childhood, we hear that the Devil is an evil danger to our immortal soul. But who is this being? Researching some of the many names the Devil has had over the millennia, I discovered some interesting facts. Almost all of the Devil's identities represent some defeated nation's God, Goddess, or protective deity. Take for instance three of the most common names for the Devil: Lucifer, Satan, and Beelzebub.

Originally, Satan personified a beautiful, radiant, and pious angel. His first appearance in the Hebrew Bible is as a heavenly prosecutor who tests the loyalty of Yahweh's followers by making them suffer, such as in the story of Job. At some time before the arrival of John the Baptist in the New Testament, Satan was changed into a malevolent entity. Interestingly, he wasn't yet deformed. His later depiction as an abomination arose from early Christian teachings on suffering and eternal damnation.

It's unimaginable in our time that the leader of a failed coup would receive a kingdom for his defiance. But remarkably, along with the Devil's banishment, God gives him dominion over humanity and the lower world. There is a mysterious relationship here between the Divine and his former favorite that begs further investigation.

Lucifer, originally called the Shining One, Light Bringer,

and Morning Star, was linked to the planet Venus, historically the representative of the Goddess of Love. The Divine Feminine was and still is an intolerable concept for the patriarchal religions that came after, and so, "She needed to be put in her place." The subjugation of women, who are to this day not allowed to possess all the rights of a clergyman, shows the repressive relationship still existing between organized patriarchal religions and the Divine Feminine. Also, because the planet's orbit is irregular, making it disappear occasionally from the sky, Venus, and by association, Lucifer, have gotten reputations for deception. Consider the Devil and Eve's purported roles in the Garden of Eden.

The name Beelzebub comes from the ancient God, Ba'al Zəbûb. The name translates as "Lord of the flies," meaning that the God had the power to cast out the pests, which were long known to carry and transmit disease. After Beelzebub's followers were overcome in a religious war of conquest, Beelzebub was turned into a demon who commanded his flies to bring pestilence and sickness *into* the world. That image is the one we still carry in our minds today.

It's well-known that historical records are incomplete and biased—winners write the histories, and always in their favor. But is it possible that the story of the devil's fall from grace is completely wrong? In *Beelzebub's Tales*, Gurdjieff gives us a very different version of events. He says that Beelzebub was initially brought to serve on the dwelling place of His Endlessness because of his "extraordinarily resourceful intelligence." But, as he was still an "impetuous youth," when he saw something he considered "illogical" in the running of the Megalocosmos, he stuck his nose in where it didn't belong.

Because of Beelzebub's persuasiveness and high standing among his fellow angels, he practically brought heaven to the brink of revolution. The Lord God put a stop to the upheaval, and subsequently exiled Beelzebub. So far, this story parallels the Christian account, as told by the English poet John Milton (1608–1674) in his epic work *Paradise Lost*, widely considered one of the greatest works of English literature. It was Milton who penned Satan's infamously prideful words, "Better to reign in hell than serve in heaven."[77]

Milton tells us that God banished the Devil to the farthest reaches of the universe as punishment for his sin. In *Beelzebub's Tales*, that place is our solar system, on our galaxy's outer edge.

Milton's Devil goes on to tempt the innocent souls on Earth, and send those he's managed to corrupt to Hell to be tormented for all eternity. In Gurdjieff's story, Beelzebub is on his way back home. His youthful transgression has been pardoned because of the many valuable services he's provided to Divinity in the years following his exile. Gurdjieff's tale of sin, expulsion, and redemption reveals something significant about the nature of the Divine and the Devil.

In another book, Gurdjieff asks the question:

> Why should He, being as He is, send away from Himself one of His nearest, by Him animated, beloved sons, only for the 'way of pride' proper to any young and still incompletely formed individual, and bestow upon him a force equal but opposite to His own?[78]

Gurdjieff comes to understand that the separation is an intentional sacrifice—its purpose to create a reminding factor to continuously evoke the striving for unity. In other words, division or separation is the first step of the creative process. Take for example the following quote:

> In the beginning, God created the heaven and the earth.[79]

The Divine divides Itself into three forces to begin the act of creation. God is active, that which divides. The Earth receives the creative impulse, and the Heavens is a mysterious mitigating force around them. There is an Eastern Orthodox prayer that shows this relationship, "Holy God, Holy Firm, Holy Immortal, Have Mercy on us."

In Rodney Collin's book, *The Theory of Celestial Influence*, he describes these three forces in scientific language as a sphere, where—

> radiation and mass [are] entirely separated, the South Pole representing as it were pure radiation and the North Pole pure mass.[80]

In Orthodox prayer, the South Pole represents Holy God, while the North Pole represents Holy Firm. Around these two opposites is the sphere of Holy Immortal, containing the almost infinite variety of energy-matter combinations, resulting from the south's plunge into the north, filling the Megalocosmos with Life, Form, and Love.

WHAT DO WE OWE?

This question is hardly ever asked—except while we're waiting for a credit card invoice or utility bill to come due. Gurdjieff, however, asks it in *Beelzebub's Tales* in a chapter called "Becoming Aware of Genuine Being-Duty." The captain of their spaceship has just finished explaining about all of the discoveries and advancements made in galactic travel since Beelzebub's exile. His grandson, who's been listening very attentively, says:

> Only now have I come very clearly to understand that everything we have at the present time and everything we use—in a word, all the contemporary amenities and everything necessary for our comfort and welfare—have not always existed and did not make their appearance so easily.[81]

He concludes he must owe something for the past labors of others, and asks how he can pay back the debt. Often, we say just the opposite, "I've paid enough." Yet we've accepted an item, and payment is due. But do we know what we've received? Though this is a personal question, I'd say for starters: life, breath, free will, choice, an embryonic soul and spirit, and the possibility to live a higher and finer life.

We're all grateful for the gifts of family, friends, work, and health that we have—*There but for the grace of God go I*—but to whom do we direct our gratitude? How can we repay such kindness? Jesus said:

For I was hungered, and ye gave me meat: I was thirsty, and ye gave me drink: I was a stranger, and ye took me in: Naked, and ye clothed me: I was sick, and ye visited me: I was in prison, and ye came unto me. Then shall the righteous answer him, saying, Lord, when saw we thee hungered, and fed thee? or thirsty, and gave thee drink? When saw we thee a stranger, and took thee in? or naked, and clothed thee? Or when saw we thee sick, or in prison, and came unto thee? And the King shall answer and say unto them, Verily I say unto you, Inasmuch as ye have done it unto one of the least of these my brethren, ye have done it unto me.[82]

SEEKING THE KINGDOM OF HEAVEN

The following quote is from the Gospel of Luke in the King James Bible of the Church of England, published in 1611:

> Neither shall they say, Lo here! Or, lo there! for, behold, the kingdom of God is within you.[83]

In the same version of the Holy Bible, Matthew tells us,

> But seek ye first the kingdom of God, and His righteousness, and all these things shall be added unto you.[84]

Taken together, we're told that the kingdom is in us now, and we must seek it out to live the life we wish for. But how can we find the kingdom inside? Where do we look? A kingdom is an area of a given size and population, ruled over by a king, though its daily running and governance require many people to perform various tasks. One way to search is to think what it might mean to take one's place in a Divine kingdom. What obligations would we accept to help our king's domain run smoothly? Although the king is primarily responsible for the welfare of the kingdom, so are all his subjects.

John F. Kennedy reminded Americans and the world of this idea during his inaugural address on January 20, 1961. The newly elected American president said,

> Ask not what your country can do for you—ask what you can do for your country.

Joseph Campbell explained that the kingdom couldn't be entered from the outside because it's an internal journey. He framed the quest for the kingdom of God in his famous saying, "Follow your bliss."

> If you follow your bliss, you put yourself on a kind of track that has been there all the while, waiting for you, and the life that you ought to be living is the one you are living.[85]

In other words, when you begin to search for the kingdom of heaven, you've begun to enter it.

Bliss is having everything truly satisfying and necessary for our planetary and spiritual bodies. We've all had tastes of this, usually in early childhood. Yet Esotericism teaches that a blissful life is our birthright. One thing to remember is that nourishing our spirit takes effort, just as it does to nourish our physical bodies.

Typically, life floods us with wants and desires, feeding our inner wolf as our higher self goes hungry. It's impossible to stop the flood of voices from entering us, but we can refuse to listen to them. What we don't give our attention to will eventually wither and die, and the energy saved can be used for evolution.

When we perform even a mundane task with focus, willingness, and attention, it feeds our soul. Why? Because we're present at those times, and finer food is released by the further digestion of impressions. So oddly, energy is used up to perform a task, but making an extra effort to do it consciously, with a light heart and to a high standard, releases higher and finer energies in us. Conversely, when we complain, get annoyed, feel owed, or generally follow our lower nature's desires, we put our attention on life's wants and subsequently get drained of energy.

Putting our attention on higher wishes while doing lower tasks takes us another step farther into the kingdom.

THE HOLY FAMILY

Ms. Marija Gimbutas (1921–1994), a world-renowned archaeologist and anthropologist, was best known for her research into Neolithic-European and Bronze-Age cultures. She introduced the use of linguistics and mythology into archaeology to understand the history uncovered in traditional excavations. Using this method, she discovered that European societies in Earth's "pre-written" period were Goddess-centered. Nature as the Divine nurturer embodied the mysteries of creation, birth, and life—giving food, clothing, shelter, and medicine to humanity.

Humanity, as we know it, first appeared on the Earth approximately 3.3 million years ago, dated by the first reported use of tools. Somewhere between 1 and 2 million years ago, humans first used fire for heating, cooking, and safety. After that, there's a huge gap in our knowledge until evidence was discovered that forty thousand years ago, our ancestors understood the principles of ceramics and developed a hearth to fire clay. Twenty-eight thousand years ago, some people lived in complex structures, and had learned how to preserve and store food. The famous limestone figurine of the Mother Goddess, the Venus of Willendorf, now in the Natural History Museum in Vienna, Austria, was carved approximately twenty-five thousand years ago.

Nine thousand years ago, some homes were built of sun-baked bricks and had plastered walls and watertight roofs. Seven thousand years ago, the Egyptians divided the night and day into two twelve-hour periods. The Bronze Age began six thousand years ago. At the same time, the world recorded its first great leap in culture—the Sumerian civilization in Mesopotamia, a region of Western Asia, which includes present-day Iraq and Kuwait.

The Sumerians were the first people to develop a codified written language, mathematics, and the sciences of astronomy and astrology. Their religion centered on the families of deities, ruling together according to hierarchy and relationships that reflected daily Sumerian life.

Then along came Sargon, the first ruler of the Akkadians, a neighboring people. He'd developed things the Sumerians didn't have, such as superior bronze weapons and military tactics. Sargon also had a distinct lack of scruples in taking what didn't belong to him. He claimed Sumerian culture for his own, establishing the first empire of conquest. This was also the start of the masculine world domination and the rise of patriarchal religions.

One theory proposed by Gimbutas and others for this reversal of a previously matriarchal world is that in the beginning, men were the protectors, providers, and craftsmen. Women kept the home and were responsible for the bearing and raising of children, a mystery unknown to men. As society shifted to a more stable agrarian lifestyle, and women took more responsibility for providing food, men lost a traditional essential role. Hunting had taken up much of man's time and was a dangerous occupation. So, soon, other "manly endeavors" came to the fore, including the reciprocal destruction of neighbors, as men realized they could take what they wanted by force.

Under Akkadian rule a similar upheaval went on in religion. The Mother Goddess became a sinister figure who was denigrated and replaced by a powerful male deity. In this new society, men ruled over the heavens, the earth, and the women. These reversals had long-lasting effects on religious teachings that incorporated their stories—like the Great Flood, the Tower of Babel, and the Garden of Eden. A significant outcome of this overturning of the Divine Feminine was giving Eve the blame for Adam's fall.

Ancient teachings say that three forces are needed to create anything. One of these conducts active/masculine influence, and another conducts receptive/feminine influence. The third is a mysterious unifying/resolving influence between the other two. Theologians have twisted themselves into knots trying to teach the idea of the Holy Trinity while leaving the Holy Mother out of the equation. From the persecution of millions of women healers and midwives as witches to the current intolerant and punitive laws regulating a woman's body, dress, and behavior—the impulse to control women is Sargon still thriving in us.

The status quo of our world is a striving for domination and power that we've suffered under for more than five millennia. However, true knowledge can turn into right action with a simple application of common sense. If we wish to consciously develop our souls, we must change our ways of thinking and feeling. It's time to reinstate the Holy Mother to Her rightfully deserved place in the Divine Family—and then act accordingly.

GOOD, BAD, SIN, EVIL

Good and *bad* are the most morally burdensome words in any language. Interestingly, by definition they're not character pronouncements but measurements of quality. *Good* is to be desired or approved of—at the top of the scale. *Bad* is of poor quality or low standard. The origin of the word *bad* is thought to be the Old English word, *bæddel*, which was a "hermaphrodite, or a womanish man," an unacceptable standard of manhood in that era of English society.

The importance of being good is impressed on most of us by threats and menaces, often with religious overtones. Good behavior will be rewarded in some heaven, while bad behavior is a sin, punishable in hell or some other awful place.

Bad and *sin* are connected in our minds, but they're not synonymous. Sin is a crucial component of biblical teaching, though it may not mean what we think it does. In Dr. Nicoll's book, *The New Man: An Interpretation of Some Parables and Miracles of Christ*, he offers a very different and possibly more accurate definition of sin.

Translating from the original Greek, he found that the word *sin* came from the word *hamartia*, an archery term that meant: "to miss the mark." According to Dr. Nicoll, a man or woman cannot sin unless they're working on their wish to evolve. In other words, you can only miss the mark when you're shooting for an aim. Sin is an objective measurement of how far off we are and which way our aim needs to be adjusted. Punishment is not involved, except what we do to ourselves.

Evil has an entirely different meaning. It's no coincidence that the word *live* spelled backward is *evil*. Going in opposite directions to life is considered evil—one of the difficulties to be contended with on the Left-Hand path, which by definition goes against the flow of life. But here's a question: are salmon evil for swimming upstream to spawn?

The idea of heavenly punishment is absurd. It makes God a hall monitor, responsible for keeping humanity in line. This opens the Lord up to blame. "How could God let this happen?" and its flip side, "God will save us." Why? Are we indispensable? Have we done enough personal work and helped enough of our fellow creatures to be worth saving?

INTENTIONAL SUFFERING

Our negative imagination is an addiction. We get a jolt of nervous energy when we picture a worst-case scenario of future events that may or may not happen. As an example, if I miss a call from my son, I immediately picture in my mind's eye all the horrible things that must have happened to him because he never calls me unless there's a problem, (which is objectively untrue). I feel a thrill of dread, and I'm restless, jittery, and uneasy until I can talk to him. This common experience is negative imagination, which results in unnecessary suffering that achieves nothing but a useless depletion of energy.

What does it mean to suffer intentionally? An example is how we quit a pernicious habit. Addiction means the body has learned to depend on certain substances to feel good. It's painful to deny your body what it now desires, and you suffer. If we choose to quit a habit and willingly undergo the withdrawal to be free from its addiction, that suffering is intentional, which always has a positive effect.

Unnecessary suffering leads to a self-perpetuating cycle of negativity. Also, we mistakenly believe that we'll be rewarded for such suffering in some future life. However, the familiar saying that "Suffering is our lot in life, our reward will be in heaven," contradicts a primary tenant of Jesus Christ's teaching:

> Neither shall they say, Lo here! or Lo there! for, behold, the kingdom of God is within you.[86]

If heaven is already in us, it can't be a reward. So, what

is it? To loosely answer this question, the Kingdom of God is a state of being on a level currently above us but attainable. We are given an idea of what's involved in the biblical story of the rich man having less chance of getting into heaven than a camel has of passing through the eye of a needle. This is about being rich with vanity, self-importance, self-satisfaction, and other piquant traits picked up along the way while indulging in life's desires. Their accumulation prevents our access to the kingdom, so we must sell these things in order to enter—an act of intentional suffering for the sake of our salvation.

Habits are hard to give up because they sink physical, intellectual, emotional, and psychological tendrils into us that attach us to things we've learned to desire. The problem is not just binge-watching TV shows or eating pints of vanilla ice cream with chocolate sauce. It's consuming our "favorite dishes," as Gurdjieff called them, like: desire for power, vainglory, comfort, the sexual fantasies we enjoy while staring at someone or their picture, the intricate plots we devise to outsmart a coworker or boss, and the subtle plans we make to one-up or impress a friend or family member. These and other imaginary scenarios are the habits we gratify daily, if not hourly. They come at a very high cost, burning up the energy we need to evolve. Our inner life can be exhausting.

When we intentionally suffer by not indulging these and other equally detrimental habits, we're plugging energy leaks, which will eventually starve unhealthy behaviors to death.

Habits can't be suppressed for long. It's like trying to hold a beach ball underwater. Eventually, it will blast free. Conquering a behavior by force also invites other equally harmful behaviors to take its place. One simple example is that many people gain weight when they quit smoking. They remove the expression of the habit, but the underlying cause remains unexamined.

We are creatures of habit because they make life easy.

We don't have to constantly think for ourselves and make choices—we just do what we've always done or what everyone else is doing. Even when we know something is bad for us, we continue doing it from habit. An open-minded look at life shows that we all are this way. Why do we vote for one candidate when we know the other is better? Well, the other is not from our party or of our sex or our religious persuasion, etc.

In order to safely overcome a habit, one's mind, heart, and body must agree on working together. One way to achieve this is to have an honest conversation with all the many parts you call *yourself* and get everyone on board with your aim. Convince them that if you win, they all win—but if they win, everybody loses. It will not be easy, as there'll certainly be more than some moaning and groaning, but the more reasons one has to achieve an aim, the better the odds for success.

CHRIST DIED FOR OUR SINS

This statement has come to mean that Christ sacrificed His life to give us a clean slate, smoothing our way into heaven, as if Jesus did our work for us. This is wishful thinking.

Jesus was born in Palestine sixty-three years after Rome conquered Judea, forty-three years after the assassination of Julius Caesar, and only twenty-seven years after his adopted son Caesar Augustus was crowned the first Emperor of Rome. At that time, the Roman world was a cruel and brutal place. About a million people lived in the capital city, and a quarter of them were slaves. Also, Augustus had declared himself Pontifex Maximus, the head priest of the Roman religion, ending the centuries-old separation between church and state. Now, any religious difference became a subversive act, and vice versa.

This oppressive, greedy empire had turned its back on the Divine and forced its citizens to worship its emperors instead. People lost their faith in higher levels as religion became more commercial and corrupt. This is one reason Christ chased the money lenders from the temple. That world had lost its way, isolating itself from the Divine and creating its own spirituality based on blind obedience to and ruthless enforcement of their current religious dogma. Zealots, the radical fundamentalists of the day, were in charge of this new world order and closed mankind's side of the bridge to heaven. Into such a time our Divine Father

> sent not his Son into the world to condemn the

world; but that the world through him might be saved.[87]

Jesus Christ carried mankind's suffering and repentance with Him to the cross, and through His intentional suffering and the ultimate sacrifice of his body, reopened the way to heaven in our minds and hearts. He showed people the Kingdom in Himself, and His teachings gave the knowledge of how to cross the bridge.

Pre-official Christianity teaches that Christ came to Earth in answer to the prayers of those seeking the way into heaven—the way of inner peace, enlightenment, cosmic consciousness, nirvana, paradise, serenity, etc. Receiving this help is as possible today as it was then because the universe is still based on the principle of response to request. If we ask for Divine help, we will receive it; however, we need to righteously and persistently make our request. Quality and quantity are both necessary here.

FREE JUDAS ISCARIOT

The wildly popular Harry Potter book series gives us some of the most interesting characters in modern literature. One of these is Professor Severus Snape, potions master of the Hogwarts School of Witchcraft and Wizardry, because his true motives and loyalties are not revealed to Harry and friends until the end of the final book. Only then does he receive forgiveness from them—and from the reader—for all his past injustices. Snape's story raises an interesting question: How would we feel about him if we never discovered his inner life?

In the biblical story of Christ's Crucifixion, Judas Iscariot is in a similar role. Most people know about the thirty pieces of silver he was given to betray Christ, and the kiss on the cheek pointing Jesus out to the authorities. Yet the Gospel of John, in reporting the events of the Last Supper, seems to indicate that something other than betrayal was going on. Jesus said:

> Verily, verily I say unto you that one of you shall betray me. Then the disciples looked on one another, doubting of whom he spake. Now there was leaning on Jesus' bosom one of his disciples, whom Jesus loved. Simon Peter therefore beckoned to him, that he should ask who it should be of whom He spake. He then lying on Jesus' breast saith unto him, Lord, who is it? Jesus answered, he it is, to whom I shall give a sop, when I have dipped it. And when he had dipped the sop, he gave it to Judas Iscariot, the son of Simon. And after the sop

> Satan entered into him. Then said Jesus unto him, that thou doest, do quickly. Now no man at the table knew for what intent he spake this unto him.[88]

To reiterate, Simon Peter asks Judas, who is lying on Jesus' breast, to ask who's going to betray Him. Jesus answers, and gives Judas the sop, telling him to do what he must quickly. At this point, no one else at the table knows Jesus' intent in saying this to Judas. He knows because the instructions were whispered to him as he laid his head on Jesus' breast.

Also, "shall" is an interesting word choice. It typically means in the future, like a prediction. But it can also be said like a command, "One of you *shall* betray me." And Jesus seems to have chosen Judas to carry out this most heart-wrenching mission. What if Jesus gave Judas the sop not to let Satan in, but to fortify His most faithful friend for his coming ordeal? Judas had to be the most loyal disciple to be trusted with this onerous mission of turning Jesus over to the authorities, as it's said, to fulfill certain scriptures. Can you imagine what Judas was going through with Christ's mission on Earth at stake?

Nikos Kazantzakis (1883–1957), considered a giant of modern Greek literature, beautifully depicts this scene in his remarkable novel, *The Last Temptation of Christ*, adapted to film in 1988. Judas is in tears, begging Jesus not to make him do this heinous act, yet Christ tells him that if he loves Him, he will do it.

In May 2006, *National Geographic* published an article titled "The Gospel of Judas." They reported that an "ancient text lost for 1,700 years" confirmed, "Christ's betrayer was his truest disciple." But if we believe Judas deceived and then betrayed Christ, we cast doubt on Christ's Divinity. How could a mere mortal deceive the Divine? Yet even the poet Dante places Judas in Satan's jaws to be gnashed alive between his teeth for all eternity. Has Judas Iscariot, whose name has come to embody deceitfulness and treachery, been falsely convicted, hated, and wrongfully punished for two millennia?

The following passage comes at the end of John's Gospel, after the resurrection of the Christ. John tells us:

> Then Peter, turning about, seeth the disciple whom Jesus loved following; which also leaned on his breast at supper, and said, Lord, which is he that betrayeth thee? Peter seeing him saith to Jesus, Lord, and what shall this man do? Jesus saith unto him, If I will that he tarry till I come, what is that to thee? follow thou me.[89]

By this time, Peter knows that Judas pointed Christ out to the authorities and that, unable to bear the consequences of his act, has committed suicide. When Peter asks Jesus why Judas' spirit is nearby, Christ tells him to mind his own affair. He wills that Judas tarry till He comes. *Tarry* means to stay around—to delay leaving. I suggest that in this case it means to abide by Jesus' side until the Second Coming—easing some of the pain Judas has suffered in Christ's name over the centuries.

This idea was unthinkable for clerics, priests, and monks of the fifth century who were tasked with codifying a church-approved biblical account of Christ's crucifixion, death, and resurrection. However, to this day this interpretation of Judas' acts remains heretical teaching for the Catholic church. It's time to reconsider our prejudiced notion of Christ's truest disciple, and his *necessary* role in the Passion Play.

SUCCESSFUL PRAYER

The dictionary defines prayer as a solemn request for help, or an expression of gratitude that's addressed to God or an object of worship. This definition is misleading because it's doesn't include levels. We've convinced ourselves that we merit Divine consideration just because we're asking. It's a deep-seated belief that we can "call up" the Good Lord anytime we need something. Why would the Divine Omnipresent Endless Unibeing Creator of All interrupt His oversight of the Megalocosmos and rush to my aid? A very scaled-down analogy is a citizen of the United States of America assuming they can contact the president directly and ask for a favor. Only someone "important" to the administration would be able to get through to the Oval Office. Why do we believe it's different for Divinity? Thinking without levels has caused many people to lose faith in the real power of prayer.

Now, granted, we're all valuable to the Almighty.

> But even the very hairs of your head are all numbered. Fear not, therefore; ye are of more value than many sparrows.[90]

And yet being of "more value than many sparrows" doesn't sound like a very high estimation of worth. What makes us think we're so special that Divinity will even hear us? In Dr. Nicoll's book, *The New Man*, in a chapter titled, "The Idea of Prayer," he presents two requirements for successful prayer:

> Only persistence and intensity can cause the higher level to respond.... Understand this point clearly: the lower is not in direct contact with the higher. God and Man are not on the same level ... as the ground floor of a house is not in direct touch with the top floor.[91]

So, what kind of prayers can reach the top floor? Dr. Nicoll goes on to write:

> Only what is sincere and genuine ... can touch a higher level. For example, any trace of vanity or self-conceit or arrogance stops communication with a higher level.[92]

There's an ancient Japanese saying: *The Gods only laugh when they're prayed to for wealth.* A higher level can't hear baser wants and desires, despite the noble-sounding names we might give them. The higher only responds to the highest and finest in us—our deepest wish for ourselves, our families, and creation.

Real prayer begins with remembering your aims and efforts. That immediately raises you into a higher place in yourself. From there, you can ask for your deepest wish and promise to do all you can toward achieving that aim yourself. Remember, God helps those who help themselves. Prayers don't have to be traditional to be useful. Make up your own, as long as it's from a real wish.

> Holy God, Holy Firm, Holy Immortal,
> please help me to externally consider always, to grow my consciousness and become a useful and loving servant of Your creation.
> Please help me to overcome (what you wish to

change in yourself) and to grow (features you wish to act from more) for the sake of my parents, my children, myself, and our families.

Please help all my essential friends to achieve their aims.

Please help me become (your deepest wish) and to find and follow my bliss.

Amen

FAITH AND LEVELS

The biblical tale of the Roman centurion who asked Jesus to cure his servant gives us the definition of faith.

> Now, when Jesus was entered into Capernaum, there came unto Him, a centurion, beseeching Him, and saying, Lord, my servant lieth at home sick of the palsy, grievously tormented. And Jesus sayeth unto him, I will come and heal him. The centurion answered and said, Lord, I am not worthy that thou shouldst come under my roof; but speak the word only, and my servant shall be healed. For I am a man under authority, having soldiers under me; and I say to this man, Go, and he goeth; and to another, Come, and he cometh; and to my servant, Do this, and he doeth it. When Jesus heard it, He marveled, and said to them that followed, Verily I say to you, I have not found so great faith, no, not in Israel.[93]

Faith is belief in the unknown, with an understanding of levels. The centurion believes Christ is Divine and will be able to heal his servant (belief in the unknown). He also understands levels viscerally because of his rank in the Roman legions and the chain of command he's in. So, he knows that Christ has only to say the word and his servant will be healed. Jesus said he had seen no greater faith in all of Israel.

Today we have very negative attitudes toward hierarchy, and because of that, we lack faith. It's naive to take "all men are created equal" to mean all men are the same. This is one reason for the backlash in society today over identities. People want to assert their individuality, and their ancestors' language, dress, social customs, expressions, and manners are all a part of that identity. When those qualities are usurped by popular culture, that hereditary connection is diluted, which undermines its effect for the people and their descendants.

Gurdjieff taught that there were seven levels of the created universe, each containing the next one inside of it, like Russian nesting dolls or spheres within spheres. First is the Megalocosmos, the body of an Unmanifest Unknowable Creator. Then there are: all the galaxies within that body taken together; all suns taken together; our sun; all planets together; Earth; and finally, our moon. Part of having faith is knowing/believing that these levels also exist in us, and that we can choose to live in higher places within ourselves, closer to our wishes and to those of the Almighty.

CONSCIENCE

As consciousness is knowing all together, conscience is feeling all together. Conscience is our connection to the Divine, and as such evaluates the impressions streaming in through our five senses and those already inside us. One of its purposes is to point out when something seems likely to be untrue or not good for us. This forewarning function also reviews the screenplays spooling off between our hearts and minds, checking the content for its accuracy in the same way.

This alert to something unhelpful or dangerous won't burn out, but it will quiet if buried deeply enough under doubt, laziness, hard-heartedness, and other stifling habits. However, as we saw in Ebenezer Scrooge's visitations, conscience sometimes comes back with a bang. There are also perverse cases where a red flag is seen and dismissed. In Catholicism, this is called a sin against the Holy Spirit—the unforgivable sin.

Conscience is the bane of political advisors, marketers, advertisers, influencers, and all such who must constantly devise new ways to help people disregard these warnings without any discomfort or distress. That's the only way to get them to buy things they don't need or are harmful to use.

THE GREATEST COMMANDMENT

A lawyer wanted to test Jesus' knowledge of the Torah, the first five books of the Hebrew Bible, pivotal to Jewish teaching. When he asked which was the greatest commandment Jesus said:

> Thou shalt love the Lord thy God with all thy heart, and with all thy soul, and with all thy mind. This is the first and great commandment. And the second is like unto it, Thou shalt love thy neighbour as thyself. On these two commandments hang all the law and the prophets.[94]

Jesus answers first from strict Hebrew law, then adds that the first two commandments are alike and equally important. He teaches we must love on three levels: love God, love thy neighbor, and love thyself. But what does it mean to love God?

> People even think sometimes that it is easy to understand that one must love God with all one's heart, with all one's soul, and with one's mind, and imagine they do. They do not understand that this means . . . they must give up completely the idea that they are their own creators, realize practically, blow after blow, that something infinitely greater than themselves exists and that they are nothing. . . . Yes, people say they love God and then go and

kill one another, or talk evilly. How can that be love of God?[95]

And who are our neighbors? Certainly not all the people in our neighborhood. Many are unneighborly, and some are out to do us harm. When we think of neighbors, we think of people we've known for a long time and maybe depended on once or twice. Esoterically speaking, neighbors are our fellow travelers on the road to spiritual development; those going toward the same end—a friend along the way, so to speak. I'm commanded to love these men and women because they're in the same struggle as I am. They need and deserve my support as their efforts support me. These are essence friends—those whose actions feed our essential selves. It is of them that it's said,

> Greater love hath no man than this, that a man lay down his life for his friends.[96]

Lastly, we are told to love ourselves, but here we have a choice of which self to love. I submit that our higher and finer self deserves and needs our love.

BEWARE THE HYPOCRITE

Hypocrisy is claiming to have moral standards and beliefs to which one's behavior does not conform. For Jesus Christ, this was the greatest sin.

> The scribes and the Pharisees sit in Moses' seat: All therefore, whatsoever they bid you observe, that observe and do; but do not ye after their works: for they say and do not. For they bind heavy burdens and grievous to be borne, and lay them on men's shoulders; but they themselves will not move them with one of their fingers. But all their works they do for to be seen of men.[97]

In societal terms, Jesus is telling us to pay our taxes, but not to follow the hypocrites who set that burden on our shoulders. They brag about the good they do with the money, but mostly it funds their incompetence, corruption, and greed. Hypocritical leaders in power collect thousands of times more compensation than any constituent gets for their work, and they pay thousands of dollars less in taxes, duties, and fees.

> Woe unto you, scribes and Pharisees, hypocrites! for ye shut up the kingdom of heaven against men: for ye neither go in yourselves, neither suffer ye them that are entering to go in.[98]

This warning is to the priests, mullahs, ministers, monks,

rabbis, and other religious leaders with an economic, secular, or political agenda—usually the result of studying sacred religious texts using the lower intellectual function alone. It's easy to slip your own thoughts into the scriptures when you're not striving to apply the lessons to your being. These hypocrites twist holy script to support their skewed viewpoint. The fifth commandment, *Thou shalt not kill*, is a good example. How often is this selectively applied or forgotten altogether to support an agenda? When those so-called religious leaders pursue earthly ambitions, they can't enter the kingdom, and they prevent their followers from entering.

> Woe unto you scribes and Pharisees, hypocrites! for ye devour widow's houses, and for a pretense make long prayer: therefore, ye shall receive the greater damnation.[99]

We typically see this in the scams perpetrated on elderly people, like using formerly famous TV and movie stars known for their "honesty" to sell them things like reverse mortgages. They assure elderly viewers of the depth and sincerity of their (scripted) concern for their well-being and future security, even thanking God for the opportunity to help. The actual payment comes due after the person's death and usually falls to their heirs, saddling them with debts they must pay out of their own pockets, poisoning their relationship with their parents.

> Woe unto you scribes and Pharisees, hypocrites! for ye make clean the outside of the cup and of the platter, but within they are full of extortion and excess.[100]

This could be addressed to all organizations, societies,

and corporations that conduct their business in the dark. For instance, the entertainment industry and major league sports presenting the glowing faces of heroes to the young while covering up their stars' alcohol, spousal, or drug abuse. Or the tobacco, oil, and gas industries flooding the airwaves and internet with misinformation about the safety of their products. This deceit is rampant in groups with a polished public image to protect and maintain, including government officials and religious leaders.

> Woe unto you scribes and Pharisees, hypocrites! for ye are like unto whited sepulchers, which indeed appear beautiful outward, but within are full of dead men's bones, and of all uncleanness. Even so ye also outwardly appear righteous unto men, but within ye are full of hypocrisy and iniquity.[101]

Think of today's hidden and not so hidden persuaders: the various political advisors, televangelists, influencers, and the like who polish and spin their version of reality until it's palatable to us. It's like buying a used car with a shiny new coat of paint and motor honey in the oil to stop the engine from smoking until the car leaves the dealer's lot.

> Ye are the children of them, which killed the prophets.... Ye serpents, ye generation of vipers, how can ye escape the damnation of hell?[102]

The prophets and other "truth-tellers" of our time are under attack by those hurt by the truth. They'll spread lies and disinformation to poison facts before they can be exposed by them. This is also true of the stories we tell ourselves for why we did one thing or another, and this is the hard part. Have I seen hypocrisy in myself? For instance, have I said things that I didn't believe just to feel accepted? Have I pretended to my children that I was a saint growing up though they burn with questions about issues similar to those I wrestled with?

Everything doesn't need to have a shiny face. Children learn primarily from our struggles.

KNOW THYSELF

This maxim was purported to have been inscribed in the forecourt of the temple of Apollo at Delphi over four thousand years ago. It's a simple yet deep saying that in part means that we don't know ourselves and should strive to. There is an esoteric idea that states: *God created the Megalocosmos because He wished to know Himself*. This may be difficult to grasp because we think God is all-knowing, and we of course know what that means, so the Almighty must already know Himself. But then why create the Megalocosmos?

Most religions tell us the world was created to glorify God, but why would the Creator need to create something simply to be glorified? Isn't that vanity? If the idea that we were created in the image and likeness of God is true, that means we were created on a Divine pattern. Likewise, if *as above, so below* is true, then the desire to know ourselves was also in that template.

Maurice Maeterlinck (1862–1949) was a playwright, poet, essayist, and the 1911 Nobel Prize winner in Literature. There is a scene in his most well-known play, *The Blue Bird*, that's set in the Kingdom of the Future, where we meet all the children waiting to be born on Earth. Each child is working on some project or idea—writing, artwork, invention—something they will bring with them to Earth when they go. Esoterically speaking, this is an accurate picture of our essences before we're born. We all took on a particular task to do on Earth, something we knew would help creation. The problem is that when we arrive, we're overwhelmed by the new planetary sensations and forget our task.

Our planetary body encapsulates a particle of the Divine, animating us. Also, inside is a flaw, which we've agreed to repair while we're here. This flaw can be thought of as something the Creator wishes to investigate further and get to know better about Himself. The Megalocosmos from one point of view was created so His Endlessness could investigate *all* the aspects of being. Part of our purpose in life is to transform one particular detail or feature in the way that only we as individuals can—and then to bring that new understanding back to the Divine.

SEPARATING WHO FROM WHAT

Esotericism is dangerous. The difference between being in a school or a cult is one's relationship to the teacher. You can be on the Left-Hand path and in a school at the same time if you're there for your own reasons and on your own quest. In that case, the teacher is someone farther along in a direction you wish to travel, a position better described as an older student.

We get into trouble when we start to follow a personality instead of the way. This happens sometimes because people think they have no choice—they must listen to this person and do what they're told. If your first question isn't "Why?" and an answer is not persistently sought, you're likely in a cult. This is true for teachers as well when they stop questioning themselves, their motives, what they're teaching, and why.

> One of the dangers of being a spiritual teacher is pride... you think you are a spiritual teacher.[103]

When the teacher is mistaken for the teaching, it usually results in a cult of personality forming around them. We all know instances of this and the acts perpetrated on society's innocents in someone or another's name. If we expect our teachers to be Gods, we must be saints. In other words, we must take responsibility for our decisions and actions. It's called individual evolution for a reason.

FINAL THOUGHTS

We've been given choice, allowing us the opportunity to change the way we live. We're created with the possibility of living a fuller, more satisfying, and meaningful life. Everyone's path is different, and we all have to find our own way—the way most suited to us. That doesn't mean we have to do it all alone— because with God, one is never alone.

* * *

Change is always scary. Yet what else is life for if not to learn and evolve spiritually? It's been said that the one with the most toys at the end wins, but do you feel like a winner these days as the world implodes from that greedy philosophy? We all know that there are no luggage racks on a hearse. When we return to the starry world at the end of our journey, we bring the spiritual achievements of our life back with us, in glory of the Divine.

* * *

As we age, we get more set in our ways, and it takes more of an effort to change. Esotericism tells us to exercise all our brains (mind, heart, body, etc.) daily to achieve balance. This also keeps them hot and malleable so they can be more easily worked. My favorite saying of common wisdom is "You don't get old and stop living—you get old when you stop living."

* * *

Be serious, but not solemn, in your approach to life and work. Humor, childlike wonder, and feelings of delight go a long way toward achieving enlightenment. People cannot be coerced, threatened or beaten into evolving. Being positive lets you view the impossible as a challenge to overcome. That puts you halfway there.

* * *

We innately know that our efforts and struggles affect our children and possibly their children. However, thinking in reverse time, we can affect our parents and their parents too. Changes we make in our lives ripple through to past and future generations. When we change ourselves, we are also transforming inherited family characteristics—an added incentive to awakening.

* * *

The difference between a fool and a wise man is that a fool has to be told something a thousand times before he gets it. A wise man only has to be told five hundred times.

* * *

Did you ask yourself, "Am I here now?"

END NOTES

1) G. Gurdjieff, *All and Everything: Ten Books, in Three Series, of which this is the First Series, Beelzebub's Tales to His Grandson* (New York: E. P. Dutton, 1964), 15. (This edition includes all 1,238 pages of the original 1950 first edition.)

2) Joseph Campbell, *The Wisdom of Joseph Campbell: In Conversation with Michael Toms*, New Dimensions Radio 4-CD set (Vista, CA: Hay House Audio, 2005), CD 4, track 5.

3) Ibid.

4) Gurdjieff, *Beelzebub's Tales*, 82.

5) P. D. Ouspensky, *In Search of the Miraculous: Fragments of an Unknown Teaching* (New York: Harcourt, Brace & World, 1949), 219.

6) Gurdjieff, *Beelzebub's Tales*, 2.

7) the Holy Bible, King James Version, Matthew 7:7.

8) Campbell, *The Wisdom of Joseph Campbell*, CD 3, track 6.

9) "Two Spirits," U.S. Department of Health and Human Services: Indian Health Service, https://www.ihs.gov/lgbt/health/twospirit/.

10) Gurdjieff, *Beelzebub's Tales*, 118.

11) Matthew White, "Necrometrics: Death Tools Across History," in *Historical Atlas of the Twentieth Century*, necrometrics.com/romestat.htm.

12) Internet Pornography by the Numbers: A Significant Threat to Society, www.webroot.com.

13) Ibid.

14) Wendy Maltz, "Pornography on the Rise: A Growing Mental Health Problem," Psychotherapy Networker.org, November 11, 2015.

15) Neel Burton, MD, "Is Greed Good? The psychology and philosophy of greed," *Psychology Today*, October 6, 2014 (revised May 2, 2020), https://www.psychologytoday.com/us/blog/hide-and-seek/201410/is-greed-good.

16) Maurice Nicoll, *Psychological Commentaries on the Teaching of Gurdjieff and Ouspensky*, vol. 3 (York Beach, ME: Samuel Weiser, 1996), 988.

17) Ouspensky, *In Search of the Miraculous*, 112.

18) Ibid., 198.

19) Gurdjieff, *Beelzebub's Tales*, 62–63.

20) Avi Selk, *Washington Post* (Yahoo news, AFP article, October 21, 2017).

21) Ibid.

22) the Holy Bible, King James Version, Exodus 11:1.

23) Ouspensky, *In Search of the Miraculous*, 181.

24) Gurdjieff, *Beelzebub's Tales*, 77.

25) Ibid., 78.

26) Ibid., 386.

27) the Holy Bible, King James Version, Genesis, 1:1.

28) Gurdjieff, *Beelzebub's Tales*, 135.

29) the Holy Bible, King James Version, Luke, 15:20.

30) Gurdjieff, *Beelzebub's Tales*, 124.

31) Ouspensky, *In Search of the Miraculous*, table 8, 332.

32) P. D. Ouspensky, *A New Model of the Universe: Principles of the Psychological Method in Its Application to Problems of Science, Religion, and Art* (New York: Alfred A. Knopf, 1948), 370–80.

33) Carlos Castaneda, *Journey to Ixtlan: The Lessons of Don Juan* (New York: Washington Square Press, 1991), 234.

34) Gurdjieff, *Beelzebub's Tales*, 15.

35) Ibid., 22.

36) Jennifer K. Nelson, and Katherine Zeratsky, "Nutrition-wise" (blog), mayoclinic.org, August 15, 2012.

37) G. I. Gurdjieff, *Views from the Real World: Early Talks of Gurdjieff as Recollected by His Pupils* (London: Routledge and Kegan Paul, 1973), 40.

38) Jean-Claude Carrière, *The Mahabharata: A Play Based Upon the Indian Classic Epic*, trans. Peter Brook (New York: Harper & Row, 1987), 105.

39) Castaneda, *Journey to Ixtlan*, 42.

40) Gurdjieff, *Beelzebub's Tales*, 1183.

41) Rodney Collin, *The Theory of Eternal Life* (Boulder, CO: Shambhala, 1984), 12.

42) G. I. Gurdjieff, *Beelzebub's Tales*, 66.

43) Jeremy Hsu, "Is There Gravity in Space?," Space.com, July 27, 2009.

44) Brian Koberlein, "Why Doesn't the Sun Steal the Moon?," Universe Today: Space and Astronomy News, November 10, 2014, https://www.universetoday.com/116158/why-doesnt-the-sun-steal-the-moon/.

45) the Holy Bible, King James Version, Ecclesiastes 3:1.

46) G. I. Gurdjieff, *Life Is Real Only Then, When "I Am," All and Everything*/Third Series (New York: Triangle/Doubleday & McClure, 1975), 47.

47) Gurdjieff, *Beelzebub's Tales*, 25.

48) "The Essence of Orage: Some Aphorisms and Observations, ed. J. Walter Driscoll, *Gurdjieff International Review* 1, no. 3, (Spring 1998, revised May 1, 2000).

49) Gurdjieff, *Beelzebub's Tales*, 25.

50) Ibid.

51) Ibid.

52) Rodney Collin, *The Theory of Celestial Influence, Man, the Universe and Cosmic Mystery* (Boulder, CO: Shambhala, 1984), 236.

53) Gurdjieff, *Life Is Real*, 26–27.

54) Maurice Nicoll, *Psychological Commentaries*, vol. 4, 1335.

55) Carlos Castaneda, *Tales of Power* (New York: Washington Square Press, 1991), 229–60.

56) Castaneda, *Journey to Ixtlan*, 28.

57) Gurdjieff, *Beelzebub's Tales*, 11.

58) the Holy Bible, King James Version, Mathew 25:40.

59) A. R. Orage, *On Love & Psychological Exercises: With Some Aphorisms & Other Essays* (York Beach, ME: Samuel Weiser, 1998), 58.

60) Campbell, *The Wisdom of Joseph Campbell*, CD 1, track 1.
61) Gurdjieff, *Beelzebub's Tales*, 27.
62) Ibid., 34.
63) Castaneda, *Journey to Ixtlan*, 46.
64) the Holy Bible, King James Version, Genesis 2:18–25.
65) Ibid., 1:27.
66) Ibid., 2:22–23.
67) Kathy Reeves, "Whatever Happened to Roy G Biv?" *Our Favorite Scientific Minds Are Those We Teach* (blog), scientificminds.com, posted September 14, 2016.
68) the Holy Bible, King James Version, Genesis 2:15.
69) Gurdjieff, *Beelzebub's Tales*, 45.
70) Ibid., 50.
71) Maurice Nicoll, *Psychological Commentaries*, vol. 1, 26.
72) *Pirkei Avot: Ethics of the Fathers*, memorial edition (Brooklyn, NY: Kehot Publication Society, 2009), 1:14.
73) The Holy Bible, King James Version, Matthew 15:11.
74) Maurice Nicoll, *Psychological Commentaries*, vol. 1, 290.
75) Collin, *The Theory of Celestial Influence*, 2.
76) Campbell, *The Wisdom of Joseph Campbell*, CD 4, track 4.
77) John Milton, *Paradise Lost: An Authoritative Text, Backgrounds and Sources, Criticism,* ed. Scott Elledge (New York: W. W. Norton, 1993), line 263.
78) Gurdjieff, *Life Is Real*, 24.
79) the Holy Bible, King James Version, Genesis 1:1.
80) Rodney Collin, *The Theory of Celestial Influence*, 2.
81) Gurdjieff, *Beelzebub's Tales*, 76.
82) the Holy Bible, King James Version, Matthew 25:35–40.
83) the Holy Bible, King James Version, Luke 17:21.
84) the Holy Bible, King James Version, Matthew 6:33.
85) Campbell, *The Wisdom of Joseph Campbell*, CD 1, track 5.
86) the Holy Bible, King James Version, Luke 17:21.
87) the Holy Bible, King James Version, John 3:17.

88) Ibid., 13:21–28.
89) Ibid., 21:20–22.
90) the Holy Bible, King James Version, Luke, 12:7.
91) Maurice Nicoll, *The New Man: An Interpretation of Some Parables and Miracles of Christ* (New York: Hermitage House, 1951), 102.
92) Ibid., 103.
93) the Holy Bible, King James Version, Matthew 8:5–10.
94) Ibid., 22:37–40.
95) Maurice Nicoll, *Psychological Commentaries*, vol. 3, 916.
96) the Holy Bible, King James Version, John 15:13.
97) the Holy Bible, King James Version, Matthew 23:2.
98) Ibid., 23:13.
99) Ibid., 23:14.
100) Ibid., 23:25.
101) Ibid., 23:27.
102) Ibid., 23:31–33.
103) Campbell, *The Wisdom of Joseph Campbell*, CD 4, track 5.

Stephen Burzi was born, raised, and schooled in New York City, graduating with a Bachelor of Arts in English Literature, which he studied because "literature tells the truth about history." Since graduation—alongside a continuing study of various religions, mythologies, philosophies, cosmologies, and G. I. Gurdjieff's opus, *Beelzebub's Tales to His Grandson*—he has enjoyed a long, successful, and fulfilling career supervising large-scale commercial construction projects in the New York Tristate area.

www.ingramcontent.com/pod-product-compliance
Lightning Source LLC
Chambersburg PA
CBHW032254150426
43195CB00008BA/444